GOD IS UP TO SOME-THING

David A. Redding

WORD BOOKS, PUBLISHER
WACO, TEXAS

GOD IS UP TO SOMETHING

Copyright © 1972
by Word, Incorporated
Waco, Texas 76703

Quotations from the Revised Standard Version of the Bible, copyright 1946 and 1952 by the Division of Christian Education of the National Council of the Churches of Christ in the United States of America, used by permission; *The New Testament in Modern English* by J. B. Phillips, © J. B. Phillips, 1958; *The New English Bible* © The Delegates of The Oxford University Press and The Syndics of The Cambridge University Press, 1961, 1970, reprinted by permission. All Scripture quotations are identified in the text by name of translator or abbreviations in conventional form.

The quotation from *In the Clearing* by Robert Frost, copyright © 1956, 1962 by Robert Frost, reprinted by permission of Holt, Rinehart and Winston, Inc. The quotation from *The Family Reunion*, copyright, 1939, by T. S. Eliot; renewed, 1967, by Esme Valerie Eliot, reprinted by permission of Harcourt Brace Jovanovich, Inc.

Library of Congress catalog card number: 72–84169
Printed in the United States of America

ACKNOWLEDGMENTS

Ruth Elmquist
Donald Kauffman
Joseph Samuel McVicker
Dorothy McCleery Redding

CONTENTS

I
HERE'S HOPING

1

HOPE FOR YOU TONIGHT

The word hope *has been turning people off. Mention hope* and they make conversation about a faint hereafter. Hope has become a bad word. When the doctor calls in the relatives to tell them, "At least there is still hope," it depresses them. And when we sigh, "Here's hoping," it is about the same as crying, "We give up." Hope has been devoured by hopelessness. The continents of meaning in what was once the second Christian virtue have been washed away until the word *hope* has become wishful thinking. The *Encyclopedia Britannica* devotes columns to the subjects of faith and love but does not list hope.

The insincerity of church people is partly responsible for corrupting hope. William Graham Cole tells an apocryphal story about Khrushchev asking Titov, the Russian cosmonaut, if he saw anyone out there during his journey in space. Titov replied, "Yes, I really did see God." Khrushchev responded, "I already knew he was there, but you know our policy, so please don't tell anybody." Titov's next interview

was with the patriarch of the Russian Orthodox Church.
The father also asked the cosmonaut if he had seen God
out there, and Titov replied in the negative as he had been
told, "No, there was no God." To which the patriarch replied, "I already knew God was dead, but you know our
policy, so please don't tell anybody." [1]

That story calls the bluff of multitudes of professing
Christians. Their faith is only a front. Many Christians are
like the young girl who knew she was a Christian because
her mother told her she was.

Since the church has been exposed, "hope springs in-
fernal" everywhere else. Mankind is being exploited by a
proliferation of false hopes.

Ponce de Leon's fabled search for the fountain of youth
was a modest mistake beside our mad pursuits. God was no
sooner pronounced dead than an enormous black market in
golden calves materialized. The typical modern sales pitch
sounds disturbingly like that incorrigible windbag, Mr.
Micawber, in *David Copperfield*. Today's commercials promise paradise more profitably than yesterday's patent medi-
cine man.

Americans fool themselves into thinking that they will be
so much happier on the hill in the bigger house with the
better class of neighbors, or when George gets the promotion, or after they come back tanned from Bermuda. Millions old enough to know better allow themselves to be
further scooped into fantasy by hormone cream, silicone
injections, or a weekly horoscope reading. Couples persuade
themselves that a new baby will patch their damaged relationship. These false hopes clean the bones of their victims
as Jesus so earnestly warned in a parable: "Thou fool, this
night thy soul shall be required of thee" (Luke 12:20).

There may be wisdom among young people whose dress
and haircut divide them from the conventional organization
man. Today's rebels are not taking all the idols of their
fathers for granted. They are right to refuse the false hopes

that have warped the homes from which they came. Running away from home is better for a son than sticking with a neurotic mother who is held together by tranquilizers and endless evenings of bridge-playing desolation. Rebellion is superior to repeating tradition's parade of crimes and wars.

Yet false hopes are flourishing in the reaction the next generation is having. Adolescence is diseased by the prevalent neurosis of defiance which draws heavily on drugs. I know of a college campus where on a given night of the week the large majority of the student body could be found under the influence of drugs. This is no exception. Drugs are being pushed avidly in the junior high schools now, and even in elementary schools.

The belief that drugs bring an expansion of consciousness is as much a delusion as the misuse of alcohol and more dangerous. In a report to the American Medical Association's convention in July, 1969, psychologist Anthony F. Philip of Manhattan's Columbia College condemned this false hope:

> Drug users insist that marijuana, amphetamines, LSD and other psychedelic agents give them pleasure, a euphoria "high" and a marvelous expansion of consciousness. A growing body of medical data suggests that they are kidding themselves on all these counts. Psychiatrists and psychologists are coming to the conclusion that potheads and acidheads do not turn on simply for pleasure and thrills, but in a futile attempt to escape profound depression.[2]

A college sophomore confessed the derangement in which his trip on LSD left him. "The room began to warp. I crumpled like a paperwad. I couldn't locate myself anywhere. I was frantic with terror." Drugs have so alienated some that they could not find their way back to reality. The acidhead may be tempted to try heroin. I talked recently with one heroin addict who felt he was in hell for he had given himself so many injections he had no usable veins left.

No youth is free if he is on the rebound from the Establishment. If he is under compulsion to defy the workhouse, he is as much its prisoner as the mechanical square thoughtlessly cranking it from the inside. If whatever is "in" for adults is "out" to a youth, he is wearing wrong side out the same yoke his father wore. A false hope in reverse is still false.

Hope itself is not fake simply because the church has falsified it. I heard of a man who gave up believing in storks because of their association with a false myth. Hope is not make-believe nor fantasy just because some parents have so perverted it. Hope is not an immature Pollyanna viewpoint nor a death wish. Hope is not planting corn and praying it will come up peaches. No one knows exactly what hope is, but one way of defining it is to say that it is the faith of Abraham as it applies to me from now on. According to Calvin, "Hope is the expectation of those things which faith has believed to be truly promised by God." [3] Faith, for instance, may believe that angels have sung. Hope reasons that one day they will sing to me. I have faith that Christ came. I have hope that he is coming soon for me. I have faith in the Good News. I have hope that shortly I will receive a special delivery. As Pelegrin writes, ". . . that somehow, somewhere, there is a grail for me as there was for Lancelot." [4]

In the past we have confined hope to something for old people who were about to die. The word *hope* conjures up pictures of grandmother in a rocker with a Bible in her lap, cramming for her finals.

Yet hope does, of course, have a huge part to play as life closes. I was impressed by our then eldest Presbyterian elder who at the age of one hundred and three took out a three-year subscription to a magazine. That was not absurd. His son happened to be in the audience when I mentioned this recently. He reported that his father lived to read the last issue of that subscription.

Hope still goes to funerals. A friend of mine in his sixties, who had only one good eye, bought and learned how to fly a helicopter. He took his wife on a vacation in it, and when they lost their way in the Midwest, he dropped down in barnyards to get directions from astonished farmers. A severe stroke grounded him, and I visited him in the hospital. That afternoon the doctors had warned him that he would probably die before morning. I sat down to hear his sob story. He shocked me instead. "David, this could not have happened at a better time!" I was speechless. "That's right! I just finished my last construction job and paid off the bills. I have had a good life, and I am ready to go." That response to death's approach was the nearest to St. Paul's that I have ever heard: "My desire is to depart and be with Christ."

Hope has two faces. While we will deal with the timeless hope that all will be well one day after this is all over, we also hope that help will rush in in the meantime to rescue us from our immediate dilemma. Hope first is like an early morning exercise which is as vital to a person as inhaling oxygen. To hope is not simply to pray that we shall one day go to heaven. Hope is what gets us through the night.

Man is a traveler. Whatever else life is, it is a journey. Each wayfarer can glance back and down, but he was created to look forward. A far distant city may constitute his ultimate destination, but hope also bears on his next step.

A young friend whom I admire was roughing it alone for a few days in the outdoors he loved. He needed fresh air, and he was hoping to recapture a confidence that life in the city had recently shattered.

"I was exploring a beautiful canyon," he explained, "and suddenly realized that I had ascended a sheer wall far higher than I ever meant to do, and I was hanging precariously over jagged rocks below. Then I lost my grip and began to fall. I knew it was the end. But in a fraction of a second the strangest sequence took place. A deep sense of peace swept away my terror as though someone had spoken:

'I have already taken care of you.' Just then a juniper bush seemed to jump out and grab me. It broke my descent and saved my life."

So many of the solutions we seek cannot be postponed. Current events trap us and we cannot survive for long. Without hope we are imprisoned in these dead ends. A heavy man hurts, "Will I never be anything else but Barrel Bill?" A young wife sobs, "Am I sexually dead at twenty-seven?" A college girl whimpers, "I do not have the stamina to stand up to my indomitable mother. She insists upon continuing as my roommate, and I cannot stop her."

These vicious circles squeeze us like a tightening vise. Relief is not enough; we cry for release. Hope promises release before too long. Hope is the untiring conviction that we are not permanently locked in our various predicaments. It is the sane but suprareasonable assumption that things will work out in time as well as beyond.

A man is canned eternally in his jam until hope pries open the lid. He cannot appreciate any solution until hope prompts him of its possibility. Without confidence a mother will not tackle the problem of the mess in Mary's room. We have to have heart to make an attempt to deal with the insolent drop-out with whom Sue seems determined to go steady. Hope is the first virtue to arrive and the last to leave the scene of battle. Love could not begin nor begin again without hope.

A few years ago I was invited to be Religious Emphasis Week speaker at a small church college. It was an unnerving assignment, for Religious Emphasis Weeks were already outmoded. In addition, a high proportion of Catholics and Jews on this campus were particularly antagonistic toward a week of required Protestant services. The faculty itself was not enthusiastic. A minister encounters enough resistance when he comes girded with a warm student invitation, yet I felt I had been honored with what might well be the last such opportunity I would ever have.

On the evening of my arrival I was informed that someone had stolen all the hymnals, and I had a sinking feeling. The hymnal thief, a handsome Jewish boy, was caught and sentenced by the Student Senate to sit in the front pew in coat and tie during each service and to take notes on which he was to be examined.

I felt as though I were preaching from behind, for heads were bowed into books or laps. There was fraternity initiation humor in it, but it was wrecking me. Late the third night of this total rejection ceremony the hymnal thief taunted me, "Why don't you quit playing around with the gospel team and come up to my room tonight where the men are?" I was too numb with despair to identify his invitation as an opening, but I had nothing else to do. I dragged my feet up the stairs to the third floor to face whatever more the core of the resistance movement had in mind for me. By that time, being burned at the stake seemed preferable to being wiped out by the cruelty of campus ridicule.

I entered a room surrounded by triple-tiered bunks stacked with insubordinates glaring at me. Rows of cold eyes kept me in their aim, and they began firing their loaded questions before I reached the last empty spot which was on target in the center of the room. "The church makes me sick. What makes you pretend there's a God?" snapped my Jewish host. When one has his back against a wall or is falling down one, as the man in the canyon, one hopes against hope. I gave them my attention. It was all I had.

Strangely, the more these men gave it to me, the better we both felt. Instead of peace replacing terror, for me it was affection for my attackers intercepting my inclination to be vindictive. I entered the room angry and hurt, but that feeling went away. Something was melting our mutual animosity.

When my turn came, I found myself answering them instead of their insults. It seemed as though all I needed to

do was to go up there and be with those men while they got
things off their chests so God could move in. We were
placed under an enchantment. All I know is that it was
none of my doing. What else could have memorably en-
deared those young men to me that night? Why were they
deeply moved instead of immensely amused by Augustine's
words with which I left them? "Our souls are restless, our
souls are restless until they rest in Thee." I heard a hoarse
whisper as I walked out: "Someone slipped us something
under the table tonight." A wall as personally formidable
as the Red Sea that faced Moses had opened for me to walk
through during those last two days on campus.

Later we shall see that hope takes work, but never have I
been so conscious that friendship is an incredible gift. I
would never have suspected that that hostile Jewish hymnal
thief would turn out to be my rescuing juniper bush. He
became my friend and we began to correspond after that
week was over. He and his followers formed a fraternity
from that evening, inviting me into honorary membership.
Then he got up a petition signed by most of the student
body requesting me to come to that college as chaplain. I
too was falling down my wall, and a hand reached out in
time to save the situation beautifully.

We need not press the panic button prematurely. Our
hard times may knock us off our stationary high horse. The
pinch may be a miracle's way of getting our attention.
Often we are like the shipwrecked men adrift and dying of
thirst, crying hoarsely from cracked lips for water. When a
vessel finally came in response to their SOS, the captain of
the rescue ship shouted, "Lower your buckets and draw
your own water. You are in the mouth of the Amazon
River."

We must not allow hope to get technical. It is better not
to be too set on exactly what to hope for. Hope looks for a
way out but not for a particular way out. The mentally ill

often absolutize one pet answer to their plight. Ahab believed that harpooning Moby Dick would solve everything.
William Golding's minister had such a fixation on the spire
of the church he was building he forgot everything else. It
fell on him and killed him. The colonel in the film *The
Bridge over the River Kwai* became obsessed with the
bridge. He became fanatic in his conviction that its completion would neatly wrap up all the problems he and his fellow
British prisoners suffered in that Japanese concentration
camp. Hope that is healthy will remain open to unforeseen
developments.

Eddie Rickenbacker did not specify how he wanted help
to come when he was tossing around in his life raft in the
Pacific. He finally prayed without laying down any conditions, so that no possibilities were excluded. Food came in
the form of a gull landing on Rickenbacker's head and by
flying fish flying into the boat. He could never have pre-
dicted what he hoped for. So often that elusive answer we
seek is, as Gabriel Marcel suggests, an "undreamed-of
promotion."

My mother-in-law had just returned from surgery. Her
surgeon called us all together. "I'm terribly sorry," he said,
"but her entire abdominal area is ravaged by cancer. We did
all we could, but tragically, in the course of the operation,
we had to sever and tie off the major artery to her left leg,
so if she happens to live any longer than a few days, gan-
grene will develop and she will face an amputation of that
leg."

We were numb. None of us knew what to pray for.
Slowly my mother-in-law regained consciousness. Two days
passed. She wondered why all the attention was being given
to her left foot, although she had asked for and had been
given her complete prognosis with that one exception. She
could not understand the excitement of the young resident
a morning or two later when he found a pulse fluttering in

her left foot. The surgeon explained: "Apparently enough collateral circulation had previously developed so that the leg could manage without the artery."

No one could have hoped ahead of time for this solution which covered everything so gracefully. She walked in comfort for several satisfying months in her own home. Her subsequent death did not diminish the wonder worked. Hope had declared one of its surprise bonuses.

Hope is not solely for major crises; it is for one day at a time. When someone asks, "Who has meant the most to you?" I am tempted to drop the name of Paul Tillich or Dionysius the Areopagite, but if I were honest I would have to own up to my great Aunt Em. She was distinguished by the way she took each day as it came on the up and up. She not only had hope; hope had her. She lived into her nineties. She was one of those rare New Yorkers who took everything that befell her as a personal favor. She went deaf, so no matter what one might swear, she assumed it to be prayer. While the rest of us were all picking at the lunch tossed us in some truck stop, she was actually cutting her way through those pork chops, shaking her head in unbelief that such marvelous food was to be found in Ohio.

One time a carload of my wife's relatives arrived with Aunt Em. I was standing out in the garden to impress them and to attract some help. Everybody naturally headed for the showers except Aunt Em. She tottered out to where I stood, flopped down on her ancient knees, and began pulling weeds too fast for me. After about an hour I began to feel the effects of the fierce summer noon sun, so I started shouting to her, "Aunt Em, don't you think you had better go inside? You might have a sun stroke." After I had finally conveyed this message to most of the neighborhood, she replied, "Oh no, this exercise is exactly what I need after sitting so long in the car. It will make us hungry for supper." We were both perspiring profusely, but she remarked, almost jubilantly, "It will soak the winter's poison out and prevent jaundice." Somehow or other I had to hang on in that garden.

As soon as Aunt Em entered a house she asked, "Which way is the kitchen?" but she was one woman who would not spoil another housewife's arrangements. I doubt if any back seat could put her out of humor for long. If I teased her at bedtime, "Aunt Em, because of the mob we have staying here tonight, you will have to sleep on a floating plank in the flooded basement," she would declare, "That is my favorite way! It will be so much better for my back than those squashy mattresses."

She was no neurotic martyr although she helped rear her sister's ten children. In middle age she fell in love with and married a man she later nursed through senility to his grave. Her prayers pled for mercy on her own "multitudinous sins." Invariably she embraced unavoidable trouble with the words that became her: "This will do me a world of good."

One Halloween shortly after she and Uncle Al had set up housekeeping, the neighborhood boys smashed pumpkins from her garden on her pin-neat front porch. The sight would have sickened even an iron constitution with despair, but Aunt Em marched out undaunted into the midst of the flying pumpkins as though it had all been arranged by a higher power. The attacking forces were hidden behind her forsythia bushes. "Boys," she announced, "if you'll come up here and help me clean up this mess, I'll have some pies made for you by the time you get back from your rounds."

Suspicious heads peeked, and then seeing that little cricket of a woman already working as though it were an accomplished fact, they surrendered and joined the opposition. The pumpkin pies became an annual affair. After that, "Nobody better mess up Aunt Em's place on Halloween." She had recruited her enemies for her protection.

Not very long ago I received the word that great Aunt

Em had died. They did not send me her dying words. It was not necessary. I know them well. For I feel sure that the final words her lips would form were the ones that I had heard her use during so many of her hard times across the years. I can see her wrinkled old gray head nodding as she died: "This will do me a world of good."

Such examples of trust in the situation in which we find ourselves shine and stretch the shrunken definition of hope until it covers completely whatever is happening to us now. True hope lights the way for life like the candles the ancients wore at night on the toes of their shoes, so they could see to take the next step.

2

HOPE
OR
PERISH

One Father's Day not very long ago a dear friend of mine
took his four little children out into the woods and shot
them, then shot himself. The chief monster in the ghastly
horror of that unsuspecting Sunday afternoon was the sense
of utter exasperation my friend had over his predicament.
His life came to a grinding halt because he had reached
the end of his hope.

Last year there were over a quarter of a million known
attempts at suicide among teen-agers in the United States.
Their deaths were the work of despair. Without hope you
and I are doomed.

Men die behind the barbed wire of concentration camps
not so much from undernourishment and overwork but
from drudgery. These walking dead men dread each day.
They are men in whom hope has died; hence they soon
will die. The goners in *A Day in the Life of Ivan Deniso-
vitch* had given up to the certain doom that awaited them.
Goners still went through the motions of life, but the heart

for it was gone out of them. Their eyes and feet still moved mechanically, but it was as though their invisible lifeline had already been cut at the neck. Their movements were like the post-mortem twitches of a snake.

Ivan had no more reason to expect escape than the goners, but something breathed in him during the bleakest nights: "We'll get through it." This encouragement nerved him to sew an extra crust into his mattress. He too was starving but somehow he would wrangle a vital piece of potato in his soup next time.

At the final turn of the screw with the air around his bunk polluted by the latrine, and with his sore throat forewarning him of the flu, something kept him from turning his face to the wall. The distinction was brutally clear there behind the barbed wire. Where there was hope there was life.

Without hope a man cannot get his breath. Losing hope is like suffocation. The Russian author Anatoly Kuznetsov recently escaped from the Soviet Union. He confessed that the effect of the happiest Communist circumstances was still hopelessness. His imprisonment was subtler than barbed wire, but the havoc wrought by despair was just as devastating. Even in his prosperity he was choking to death.

> You will say it's hard to understand. Why should a writer whose books have sold millions of copies, and who is extremely popular and well-off in his own country, suddenly decide not to return to that country, which moreover, he loves?
>
> The loss of hope. I simply cannot live there any longer . . .
>
> I wrote my last novel, *The Fire*, with no feeling left in my heart, without faith and without hope. I knew in advance, for certain that, even if they published it, they would ruthlessly cut everything human out of it, and that at best it would appear as just one more "ideological" potboiler . . .
>
> I came to the point where I could no longer write, no longer sleep, no longer breathe.[1]

However, life and liberty in the West could dash Kuznetsov's hope as nicely as Soviet censorship, according to our

contemporary writers. People on and off campus here as
well as in the Far East have fallen in love with hopelessness. Look at our literature. Atheist existentialists such as
Jean Paul Sartre make their livelihood preaching the philosophy of despair.

American newspapers are fat with examples of Pro-
methean despair, the despair of presumption. Many men
have despaired of a creative solution and have resorted to
pressure. This is the despair of the powerful and one need
not go to the Kremlin for it. The tragedy at Kent State
University will do, and so will the muffled gunshots of the
Mafia and the malicious epithets of the black or white, left
or right militants.

A more menacing despair may be that of Sisyphus, the
despair of the trapped. Their futility has created the Theater
of the Absurd to which *Waiting for Godot* may still be the
best introduction. Samuel Beckett's characters cannot complete sentences nor make sense and keep forgetting the
names and faces of their friends. Godot never comes and
they don't care.

Despair rips with a vengeance from the happenings of
Jean Jacques Lebel. He stages the crucifixion of a chicken,
contemptuously flinging its spurting parts into the faces of
his audience. Despair is busily writing the requiem of art.

The affluent society is driving the next generation to
desperation. Parental pressures seem to be pushing youth
to bizarre extremes. Youth is reacting negatively to a way
of life that offers them no hope of fulfillment. Their hostility
to our hygiene is their way of thumbing their noses at a
home that has alienated them, giving them things instead of
attention.

The heart goes out of a family if the father is owned by
his company. One executive's wife of forty-one was forced
to tear up her nest for four in order for her husband to
receive more pay on the West Coast. They could see the
blue ocean from their brutally new 450-dollar-a-month
view, but the wife broke down. Without the familiar faces

and the place she had made for herself in Pennsylvania, the reassuring friend she went with everywhere, she was lost. Her telephone bills back East during the first month ran into hundreds of dollars.

The pressure to succeed in school and sports also dampens the spirits of the susceptible. The hopes of many of our young people are wiped out by the competitive system. It is as though the boy were made for the job, for the game, or for the grade, and he's out if he cannot measure up.

A college football player with an arm in a sling approached his coach, a former pro whom the player obviously adored. The big guy questioned the coach in front of a number of students standing around in the snack bar. "Coach, how soon do you think I will be able to come out for practice again? I get this cast off Monday." "Denny," the coach thoughtlessly blurted out, "Art and I had a talk about you, and we decided that you don't have the bones for football. This is your second fracture, and we are dropping you from the squad."

No one could have better brought disaster on that boy. His idol had brutally broken his dreams in front of everybody. The coach was not mean, but he had callously performed the major surgery of removing this boy's hope as though it were only a stick of gum. After fumbling a few phrases in a vain attempt to conceal the extent of the wound he had suffered, the lad disappeared downtown and didn't come back.

Instead of destroying him in public, the coach should have stood by the boy in private to see that his hopes were safely transferred to the sport that suited him. This is to say nothing of the command given to all of us to secure each other to the "sure and certain hope" that can sustain us through all our ups and downs. Obviously this boy had been denied this deeper virtue, or he could have survived this relatively minor disappointment.

The most hallowed halls of learning can be the site of

one's execution as well as any firing squad. One promising young English student finished his first semester of graduate work with a private promise that upon completion of his Ph.D. he would receive an assistantship in the English department of his first choice school. He dreamed of little else. Literature was his life. He had taught it for several years. Fortified with excellent marks in his two other courses, he went into an interview with his favorite professor in his third course. This particular small seminar was open only to candidates for the Ph.D. degree and accounted for half of his semester's credits. Anything below B was unacceptable.

Without any warning the young man walked into disaster. His professor was irrevocably disgusted with his paper. The professor brandished it, demanding to know how any student had the gall to submit such illiterate workmanship. "I checked your quotations at the library. You cannot even copy a quotation correctly. I find I cannot trust your references. You are not only careless but you lack integrity." The professor looked at his victim with loathing and ended the interview exhaling smoke in his face and shouting, "Get the hell out of the field of English!"

Looks can kill. Numb with unshed tears of rage and shame the demoralized student stumbled from the office. His colleagues asked him the results of the interview, but hopelessness held him mute. The professor had wiped him out by wiping out his future.

How different the story would have been if, instead of showing exasperation, the professor had extended his confidence in this promising student by allowing him to rewrite his paper or by seeing him through the huge adjustment he would have to make to survive emotionally. He could have handled the interview as a friend rather than as an executioner. The professor had presumed to judge his motives instead of teaching him how to do research.

A lovely high-school senior stopped me after worship at a summer church conference. "I must tell you something that my parents would never understand. They have dreamed for years of my going to the eastern college my mother and her mother attended. Until last year my grades were high enough to satisfy them that I would be eligible. But a few weeks ago in the midst of my math final, I realized I was flunking. Knowing that my parents would never be able to tolerate my failure, I cheated and I was caught. Knowing also that my parents could not possibly tolerate that humiliation, that night I took what is supposed to be the fatal number of sleeping pills. For some reason I lived, although I felt terribly sick the next day. My parents believed that I had the flu.

"I know that suicide is wrong, but except for a confidence which has come to me at this conference, I think I might have gone back home and tried it again."

One cannot take a step, read a line, wash his face, or smile good morning without hope that it is worth the effort. This is true for anyone no matter which side of the iron curtain or the tracks he is on. When someone loses morale he cannot lift a finger and finally fades into a dark corner of the mental hospital. Hopelessness comes when one cannot summon the will to live nor the will to die. Perhaps the picture of the desperate is not of the corpse but the catatonic.

At the bottom of the pit may be the bored. This is the way the decent man despairs. He is too proud to admit his hopelessness even to himself. It is supposed to be good form to grin and bear it. When one represses his specific reasons for wretchedness, they return to haunt him as unidentifiable depression. He tries in vain to distract it by being perpetually on the go or always ready with a joke. Here is where despair reaches epidemic proportions. Millions of speeding Americans are numb with apathy. They are dead to their world. Life is earnest, but life is not real for them. And it is no fun.

No wonder that hope is a commandment and that hopelessness is blasphemy. The first commandment requires confidence in the God who thought his creation a good idea.

All ten commandments oblige us to be loyal to life. Jesus never denied life's ambiguity. He simply denied the right to despair: "Only believe." Jesus so often commanded his patients to have faith. Despair is not an act of intelligence but a spell of witchcraft. To insult the longstanding summons to exist is to be out of order and to attack God. We are not consulted on this big question of whether or not to breathe. Life offers us no choice but to hope: "I have set before you life and death, blessing and cursing; therefore choose life." And so, as Will Durant has written: "From Navgorod to Cadiz, from Jerusalem to the Hebrides, steeples and spires raised themselves precariously into the sky because men cannot live without hope."

II

DOORWAYS
TO
HOPE

3
YOU CAN'T DO IT YOURSELF

Hope flowers from friendship. Hope does not burst from a solo do-it-yourself kit. Each man needs privacy and plenty of elbow room, but trying to be a self-made man is a setup for disillusionment. We must have mothers and friends to whom the egotist in us can boast about what we imagine we have done all by ourselves. "Male and female created he them," and every baby that is conceived is born from a family of relationships. The hope of the sleeping princess waited for a kiss.

A friendless man cannot enjoy self-confidence. One lacks the heart for life until someone loves it into him. The initial lift to our bootstraps must be exerted from the outside. Hope enjoys good company; otherwise a man is coffined in solitary confinement.

Perhaps there are some who profit from the tiresome refrain to put legs on their prayers, but many suffer from that advice. We need to luxuriate in the good news that there is more to prayer than legs. It is permissible to request

33

a hand. Good neighbors are a necessity not so much for their assistance as for communion.

Hopelessness is a sob story of gross neglect. Adult depression often results from having been marooned as a child to second place in a fine family. The initial reception one receives in this world determines his eventual capacity for clinging to hope.

That young father who killed his four children and then himself suffered from a sense of futility that had festered in him from the cradle. He could never please his father, not even with his gifts. His memory was raw with instances.

Etched upon his mind to the day of his death was his memory of racing down the stairs one Christmas morning only to discover that his stocking was stuffed with coal. This cruel trick was delayed punishment for forgetting where he put his boots two weeks before. That rejection on Christmas morning crumpled him into a ball of discouragement. He spent Christmas under his bed. Such isolating experiences permanently dampened his spirits. This boy never got over the effects of the way they walked on him. Beside the word *father* on his last Christmas list he had scrawled the word *nil*.

A little boy used to lie across the railroad tracks until the last minute before a train came. His eyes were desolate. Rope was one of his favorite playthings, and one day they found him hanging from a beam in a deserted warehouse. He had been an emotional cast-off. His father was gone in the morning when the boy awakened and returned home at night after the lad was in bed. His mother abhorred him from behind forced smiles. He was kept out of the way as much as possible. He became a pest. No one bothered to discipline him.

One night he went after the baby sitter with a belt. She enforced discipline but was drawn to the unhappy little boy. She sat beside him on the bed in the dark. "Honey, won't you tell me what is wrong? I want to be your friend." At

that he began to sob. "No one wants me around. I don't
have any friends. No friends at all. No one loves me." It
was not long afterward that he took the rope and made his
last trip to the warehouse. He had concluded that anything
would be better than the wretched desolation in which he
had struggled in vain to exist.

A woman in her fifties was still dispirited from the rough
treatment her parents had administered. She recalled the
unhappy day when as a child she was clutching the cuffs of
her father's trousers frantically begging his forgiveness for
something evidently so unmentionable that he would not
even explain what she had done. He shook her off in disgust
with "Get the hell out of here!" Hope leaks fast through
little fingers not held fast by love. Hope cannot last unless
someone's love lances that wound and makes up for the
deficiency later on.

Yet the wrong kind of love stifles hope. A man's depression is as often due to a mother who won't let him go as to a
father who forgot to come home from work.

The unhappy young man in *Arturo's Island* by Elsa
Morante began to grasp what hamstrung him in despond-
ency. The villain was his inescapable mother.

> When she can't enslave you she cheers herself with the
> old tale of the martyred mother and the heartless son . . .
> everything around her is soaked with tears . . . the minute
> you turn up, she starts accusing you in the most high falutin'
> Biblical way. The mildest insult is *frightful murderer!* Not
> a day goes by without her chanting this litany. Maybe she
> hopes to make you hate yourself with all these accusations,
> to rob you and set herself up as a gloomy usurper of all your
> glory and your pride. Wherever you escape to—miles away
> into town—you can't escape that everlasting parasite, her
> love . . .
> . . . and so, the whole creation threatens to turn into a
> cage. That's all that love of hers dreams of, what she'd really
> like would be to keep you always a prisoner, the way you
> were when she was pregnant.[1]

A mother can so impress upon a son that doing good means pleasing her that he feels guilty ever after for having any wishes of his own. He is reproached so decisively for showing any independence from her neat programming that even after he is grown and she is dead and gone he cannot say no to any requests without feeling unbearably guilty.

The youngster who has been possessed by such warped love, like the youngster who has been dispossessed, tends to be emotionally trapped into going along with the crowd no matter how unfair this is to his dearest wishes. His strait jacket may ache so much from his having repressed himself that his despair becomes disguised by boredom. He finds nothing really interesting because he has been submerged in someone else. He has never been allowed to stand up and identify himself and his own interests. The battle with boredom, as Father Lynch illumines it so eloquently in his *Images of Hope*, "is a battle between human beings . . . the other human being may not be there. He or she may even be dead; but the past and the dead are incorporated into the sufferer." [2]

Jonathan Winters, the comedian with cheek, was marrying Phyllis Diller of the electrocuted hair in the film *Eight on the Lam*. He also played the part of his heavy-handed mother who was anchored prominently in the foreground of the wedding ceremony, her face quaintly framed with iron-gray hair and fenced with antique spectacles near the ridge of her formidable nose.

The minister asked Jonathan, "Will you take this woman to be your lawful wedded wife?" Before the groom had time to respond, his mother took the initiative from him and dogmatically answered for him, "He will!"

"Ah, Mom," complained the interrupted groom, "I wanted to handle this all by myself." The old girl snapped back, "I was only trying to do my duty as a mother." Then the bride punctured the reigning queen with the pertinent question, "When do you go off duty?"

Such a mother must go off duty not so much for her daughter-in-law's sake as for her son's sanity. He must disassociate himself from her until he assumes command of himself. Then his attentions to her will be under his management and not produced and directed by the tyranny of her threats and tears of self-pity.

As Freud found, those who stepped on us in the past may remain standing there until someone on our side helps us pull them off. Time will not heal nor reactivate our will to live. Only true love can make it up to us. We must find a friend who will pick this burden off our backs, this oppressive reminiscence we cannot quite detect or move alone. Friends must undo what enemies did. "Hope is an act of the city of man."

Mean men were not born mean any more than mean dogs. Only mistreatment makes mean dispositions. An act of spite is an act of desperation and is often one's only strategy against the domestic villainy that put a stone in his stomach instead of his birthright of bread.

If someone has stolen hope from us, we must look to someone else to retrieve it. "Hope happens," Marcel writes, "in the department of us," when fresh friends offer us the elbow room to be ourselves that others have denied us. Sigmund Freud decided that men were cured by honesty while Martin Buber credited the relationship between the therapist and the patient.

The task of therapy is to help the sufferer to pin the blame where it belongs. To accomplish such candor requires a deep bond between listener and speaker. Buber believed rightly that this involves more than a one-sided transference; it requires reciprocating friendship. When the victim brings those offenders responsible for his troubles to justice before his counselor, at the same time indulging the tears and rage that have been checked until then, he removes the sting. Insight and relief rush in. The experience enables him.

A slight, painfully shy but fine looking lad visited my office. He had exhausted every prospect of handling his distress single-handed. He sat down quietly and was soon sobbing. He wore a black patch over one eye. Neither of us spoke for the longest time.

At last he explained between sobs, "What bothers me most is that I don't know what other people think about me. I can figure them out, but I don't know where I fit in, or what they expect of me. Kids have stared at my patch as long as I can remember. I could have been rid of it by now but my father put off the operation.

"My brother and I are twins. My father always treated us as one when it came to punishment, but my brother received all the praise. He was popular and his grades were good. When the kids on our street chose sides to play ball I was always the last to be picked. If there happened to be an odd number, I was the one who was left out. The only friends I ever had I got through my brother. My father wouldn't let me play outside one night because for once my brother flunked a test. My father and I had a big argument for I didn't think it was fair, but I lost and had another relapse. My father forgave me, finally."

It was as though the boy had finally found his tongue to tell his side of the story, squelched until then.

"One time I got a new basketball," he went on, "and I decided to go up to the park and try it out, but some boys from the accelerated program were there. They took it away from me, and I tried and tried to get it back but they kept knocking me down. Finally I went to one of their parents. It seems as though I have always had to go to extreme measures just to get what was supposed to be mine."

This young man was stuck in his emotional circle until he found someone who would listen and let him cry his way out. He could never savor self-confidence nor look forward without dread until he could discharge that backlog of unresolved grievances. He did not need advice. He needed to disgorge, to digest, to be drawn out, and to discover his own counsel. He certainly did not need more pressure to put out more effort. He was too conscientious. He had not only been bridled, he had been bottled. It was his turn to recollect and correlate in the presence of someone who appreciated him, an experience which would pave the way for him to appreciate himself.

Someone had to stand in and make up for the failure of that father. The boy needed a working surrogate to work out the unfinished business of his boyhood. Perhaps his brother should have been restrained, but this twin was still waiting to be freed from his father's vise so he could be free to be himself. Every boy needs an appreciative mother and father. Failing this, his future and his outlook on the future depend upon his doing his catching up in the hands of a replacement.

> That is one great desideratum for the sick, to find a point of pause or rest or peace in a person who does not strike back, who brings the endless battle to an at least temporary halt. The religious representation of this relationship is contained preeminently in the image of Christ.[3]

Bill, another college student, was suffering a severe depression. He could not study. Finally, under the pressure of deadlines for work already overdue, he could not bear to attend class. He stopped eating and stayed in his room for longer and longer periods. Then he began locking himself in. He lacked the energy to execute a suicide plan.

A well-meaning professor gave Bill a good talking-to. A sympathetic fraternity brother tried to arrange a blind date. The college physician prescribed a stimulant. Bill was actually dying of despair, and all these Band-Aids of good ideas for Bill were of no use until someone went to the bottom of his trouble and opened the drain.

Bill's despair did not just happen; it was compiled from a secret album of painful occasions. Specific reminiscences were flooding him with waves of despair. Until those particular abscesses were located and lanced, Bill would continue to be a basket case. Without outside help he would be too preoccupied with his unidentified emergency to have time for work. His bind was rapidly becoming an extreme example of the kind of anxiety that plagued Anna's deserted son in Tolstoy's *Anna Karenina:*

> . . . he was far more capable than the boys his teacher held up as examples . . . the boy, his father thought, did not try to learn what he was taught. But as a matter of fact, he could not learn it. He could not because there were much more urgent claims in his mind than those which his father and his teacher made on him.[4]

Hope for Bill came through the personal interest a beloved old dean took in him. The dean's interest was not clinical nor calculated. He was drawn to the boy and he saw the makings of a man in him. The dean was not a Dutch uncle, and he knew better than to paralyze the boy further by applying any more pressure. Bill knew instinctively that the dean was not trying to maneuver him. The older man possessed a contagious low-key confidence that things were going to work out. This made the difference for Bill.

The dean met with the youth frequently but seldom spoke more than a few sentences. Such affectionate quiet attracted Bill's anguish to the surface, and he was soon crying out what was wrong. His torment had made him mute until someone would hear him out without interference. As Kierkegaard perceived before Freud, so long as his suffering remained a secret it would continue to keep him in its power.

Bill's big burden was that he had come after his brother

in his parents' affections. The role of the unblessed boy can be far more demanding than being condemned to hard labor. "They always gave me the same size piece of cake, but my portion came with a nod while my brother's had the family's hopes pinned to it. He got his share because he was the favorite. I got mine because it was only fair."

The dean's compassion wrenched the jagged pieces from him. Bill was not crying crocodile tears nor getting into the habit of self-pity. He was breaking through the emotional stumbling blocks to his vocation once and for all. One never knows how much time each individual catharsis and healing takes, but it will not need repeating.

Something had happened when Bill was eight that he could never before bear to remember. Slowly the painful scene rematerialized in his mind. "I was standing in the back yard with my father's hammer in my hand. My little brother ran into the house holding his head screaming. My mother opened the screen door for him and swept him into her arms looking panic-stricken. Then she saw me standing there with the hammer. She yelled for me to come in, and then she disappeared into the family room, grabbed the ivory-handled bull whip that decorated the wall, and came for me. I was so scared I couldn't move or speak. I thought she was killing me. I knew she wanted to, and I felt dead inside.

"A few minutes later my mother found a honeybee sticking in my brother's hair where she thought I had hit him. She finally muttered, 'I'm sorry,' but she never came near me." Bill's head dropped in his lap. "I feel guilty for even mentioning this against my mother."

One night not long after that incident he realized he was having a nightmare. He screamed hysterically for what seemed hours for his mother or father to come and kiss him good night. No one came.

His mother's unconvincing "I'm sorry" did not erase the swelling sense of injustice that years of such unfair discrimination had branded into Bill. His gloom had been gathered from a history thick with such cutting reminders of his parents' preferences for his brother.

When Bill arrived from prep school for his first weekend at home, his parents' greeting ground into him like glass: "When are you going to get a haircut?" No one hugged him or kissed him; no one mentioned that he had been missed. His prep school commencement slipped by without any celebration for several unconvincing reasons. The banquet boasting his brother's graduation worked out without a hitch.

Bill felt much better after pouring out his inside story to the dean. With the negative out of the way he was able to think about something constructive. His improvement did not come neatly nor overnight, but he felt freed and nerved to act. Each succeeding move he made brightened his spirits.

The first step for any emotional sufferer is this confession of wrongs others have perpetrated on him, probably before his guard was up. The contemporary mood of much psychology is to deal only with present difficulties, but from my experience Freud was right in believing today's difficulties are distorted by yesterday's unattended grievances. We cannot forgive and forget until the oldest bones are no longer sticking inarticulate in our craw.

This initial step in self-acquaintance and acceptance must be taken as soon as friendship permits in order to clear the deck for action on current events. Doing our first job on ourselves prevents the familiar tragedy of someone projecting upon another or upon a social cause his own unresolved complexes. Unless we can see daylight in our own lives and enjoy a reasonable promise of fruitage there, we will be driven to escape into our professions or to meddle in someone else's business.

Such a frustrated person becomes a frenzied pusher, forces things to a head prematurely, and has a tendency to be a fanatic. The man who has gained self-composure and is reasonably at rest deep within himself will be able to create unity and serenity among others.

Perhaps Bill may never become secure enough to be able to mend others as the dean had done, and yet the older man's life showed remarkable similarities to Bill's, and he too had enjoyed a key friendship such as Bill enjoyed from him. Great men often found their way through friends who had in turn been so befriended. Remember that murderer Moses, that adulterer David, that enemy of Christ named Paul, and the Simon Peter who betrayed the Master three times? The reclamation of all is a study in friendship.

Hope can come late in life to the desperate. Gert Behanna, who inherited two fortunes and married two more, confessed her flamboyant descent in the wasteland of friendlessness in her striking recording, "God Is Not Dead." Though she had everything she had nothing, for she had no friends. Her isolation was soaked in alcohol and spiked with drugs. Not satisfied with this self-inflicted slow torture, one night she took several times the lethal dose of sleeping pills, but lived to tell the lurid tale of *The Late Liz*.

Since she failed even as a suicide, Gert found herself at a famous clinic. After thorough examinations the doctors humiliated her further by saying that they could find no organic reason for her problems. The interviewing physician pushed a piece of paper across the desk toward her. "Here are the names of the only two men in the country who might help you." Both were psychiatrists. Gert stumbled from the consultation room and, to her great amazement, found herself pronouncing a word she had never said before except in profanity. "I don't need a psychiatrist," she said. "What I need is God."

The nearest person Gert had to a friend lived in New York. She begged to introduce Gert to a couple she knew who had been like Gert but who had been converted. "Converted to what?" exclaimed Gert. "I had a convertible automobile." "I mean, Gert, that their lives were rather like

yours and their faith changed them." Gert consoled herself
with the thought that since the suggestion came from someone who did not eat peas with her knife these people would
not be barbarians. She fortified herself with alcohol to face
her first two Christians. She addressed them indulgently in
baby talk. "So God speaks to you, does he? Now tell me,
what did he say?" The couple were not put off by Gert's
maudlin reception. "Gert, you do have problems, don't you?
Why don't you let God take care of them?" "You make it
sound as though I had too many suitcases to carry, and
needed a porter." "That's about it." Gert was disarmed by
their patience.

She drove home in her air-conditioned Continental and
received the shock of her life. Waiting to welcome her was
a momentous letter from that couple, the first real friends
she ever had: "We are praying for you each day . . ."
"Praying for me?" Gert exclaimed. "I could never remember anyone ever caring enough about me to do that." An act
of friendship at this crucial time gave Gert the heart to give
God a try. She fell to the floor by her bed and cried, "Oh
God, if you are anywhere about, I hope you'll help me, for
I sure need it."

"In twenty minutes," she said, "it was all over." The late
Liz was gone and a new woman had taken her place. Gert's
momentous transformation had been waiting for two friends
to go a tiny timely second mile.

Hope springs too from the last full measure of devotion.
Presbyterian missionary Irene Forsythe was sentenced to
public denouncement and trial in a village square shortly
after the Communist takeover in China. Usually the mobs
made bloody work of the charges trumped up by the shrieking puppet officials. The day of reckoning approached. Irene
prayed against the inevitable.

On the night before her denouncement, without any ex-
planation Irene was quietly slipped aboard a vessel bound
for New York City. When she docked she discovered that

the secret of her rescue was a Methodist missionary named
Hansen whose wife had died in a Communist prison. Dr.
Hansen had volunteered to take Irene's punishment without
her knowing it. Then for no apparent reason, Hansen himself was abruptly released and by a shorter route had reached
the dock in New York in time to greet Irene. In the States
Irene learned that a friend had felt prompted to pray for her
around the clock during the last day or two of her imprisonment. Before long she and Dr. Hansen were married. One's
encouragement comes often through another's sacrifice.

Despair descends on us when we are left out; it leaves
when love moves in. The one true friend removed the cross
of despair from off our backs. "Greater love hath no man
than this . . ." (John 15:13a).

What a friend! He was the first of the friends that can
forgive and understand without any conditions. The God
who helps those who help themselves is either a monster or
a mouse. Whatever else God is, he is a friend who helps
him who has no helper. No doubt the Atonement of Christ
has been abused as a labor-saving device as Danelieu has
observed, but what makes the Savior a savior is not that he
upstaged us all. He steps down into the shoes of another
man's otherwise inextricable predicament. He does not mo-
nopolize his contribution; he makes us partners.

T. S. Eliot's words in *Family Reunion* are reminiscent of
David's thanks to Jonathan, the orphaned Lincoln's to
Nancy Hanks, or yours and mine to the one who introduced
us to him "who for us men and our salvation came down
from heaven":

> Of a door that opens at the end of a corridor,
> Sunlight and singing; when I had felt sure
> That every corridor only led to another,
> Or to a blank wall.[5]
> You bring me news

4

THE TRUTH
WILL
FREE
YOU

"The truth will make you free." Freud unwittingly founded psychoanalysis on this verse of Scripture. William F. Lynch, an eminent psychologist, likes to say: "The bare facts will free you." [1] Any ex-prisoner of fantasy can prove it. Seeing ourselves as we really are and telling it like it is invites hope. It is impossible to have happiness or hope of it without being in sure possession of our facts and faculties.

The man who fools himself finally becomes as despondent as the one whose parents tricked him for he cannot even depend upon himself. He is wrecking his peace of mind and frustrating his chances of fulfillment. Inflation of the facts never brings any cheer. If a man is feeding himself a line he is alienating himself in no man's land.

The less one looks life squarely in the face the more likely he will suffer delusions of grandeur or even hallucinate. These makeshift defenses will not secure hope. Lies breed lies until the collection at last collapses under its own dead weight. Living a lie is the last strategy a hopeless man uses.

46

He has already lost that precious capacity to appreciate things straight, a capacity which we call sanity.

We have long since stopped beating and chaining the pitiful victim of hopelessness although our mental hospitals still quiver from the force of brutal chemicals and charges of high voltage. What we are more concerned with is that appalling strait jacket a man pulls on himself when he begins giving himself the benefit of the doubt so recklessly that he flaunts the facts. As circumstances squeeze him, he builds higher and higher castles in the air.

Instead of bringing relief his escape mechanism becomes exhausting, for he must keep tacking this unworkable world together. The cost of the effort is enormous. Trying to make the impossible possible is strenuous to say the least. To whatever degree a man descends into self-deception, he cuts himself off from his only life. Complicated and constant re-shuffling is required of anyone living in two worlds, especially when he must make them look like one. He is forced to come up with excuses for the maddening and multiplying questions. Each yarn he spins straps him down further until he is hopelessly bound hand and foot. He cannot find his way out of his fairy tale.

There are many mad men who lug their bitterness from old sores and blame it on new and innocent situations. Often this self-deception originates in a long-term protective device adjusted in childhood.

> Such fantasy, in terms of which so many people must work, is expressed in the classical psychiatric joke of the man whose car broke down, and who found himself trudging with his own thoughts toward a farmhouse a mile away, to ask for a jack. The image of the hypothetical farmer and his anticipated refusal grew in his mind as he walked. When he knocked at last on the farmhouse door he heard himself yell out: "You can keep your blankety blank jack." [2]

Such persons cannot distinguish between their imaginative memory and what faces them. Hope for them lies in their

being able to fix the blame where it belongs. When the
confused is able to be brutally frank blow by blow, he can
be healed and can hope again. Freud likened the process of
psychoanalysis to the unearthing of a buried city, and his
first patient called it "chimney sweeping." Both analogies
underscore how integral absolute honesty is to therapy.
There is no way out of one's predicament other than by
knowing the truth, and for so many people, specifically
coughing up the truth word for word. Once one attends to
what has happened, his attention is free to look forward.

We must be honest with each other, too. A wife's heart
was broken by the affair her husband was having with another woman. To her surprise she knew her heart was
broken before she knew why. She had been sobbing herself
awake each morning for weeks before she had the slightest
conscious knowledge that anything was wrong. Her husband's dishonesty affected her as soon as it existed, and she
was relieved as soon as she knew. When we tell someone an
untruth it immediately arouses anxiety in them. They may
not identify the falsehood, but dishonesty undermines rap-
port.

So often the family naïvely assumes it does the hospital-
ized member a kindness by keeping any bad news from him,
but actually what the patient doesn't know will hurt him.
"Joe, you are getting better and you will be walking out of
here before you know it." If that statement is false it will
have an adverse effect on Joe. He may not notice its hollow
ring. He may not consciously suspect its truth. But for some
reason, the statement carries no weight. It does not cheer
him. Despite the gay words he feels worse. If that artifi-
ciality continues, he begins to feel excluded and isolated. He
becomes too anxious to relax. He is increasingly nervous and
fretful.

The truth should not be forced on Joe, but the dying man
who is being teased with white lies dies a thousand deaths
compared to the man who can trust his loved ones and who

is able to pass around the pain and the awe of dying. We torture the patient when we make him an outsider to his plight. He is comforted when he has the facts and has someone to keep him company during their digestion. Hope is jeopardized if the patient excludes his friends from his feelings. If the night before the operation he pretends a brave front, denying his friends and himself an acknowledgment of the actual state of affairs in his fears, he suffers far more than another patient who frankly exposes his chicken-heartedness. Under the anesthetic the truth comes out—the pretender's panic, the honest man's composure is exposed. Reality relaxes one and creates promising conditions. Candor is the only way to make friends with the situation and with God. One is so often the cowering slave of his secret.

Our daily deceits not only dishearten us but can actually give us a heart attack. While frankness in personal relationships is an area that requires great tact and delicacy, a growing number of physicians are commenting on the damage deception does to our bodies. Boris Pasternak diagnosed this in *Dr. Zhivago:*

> Microscopic forms of cardiac hemorrhages have become very frequent in recent years . . . It's a typical modern disease. I think its causes are of a moral order. The great majority of us are required to live a life of constant, systematic duplicity. Your health is bound to be affected if, day after day, you say the opposite of what you feel, if you grovel before what you dislike and rejoice at what brings you nothing but misfortune. Our nervous system isn't just a fiction, it's a part of our physical body, and our soul exists in space and is inside us, like the teeth in our mouth. It can't be forever violated with impunity.[3]

One of the encouraging recent developments in Christianity is the retreat into small groups where men and women can go behind the artificial front lines life has been tightening on their faces to the real lines of struggle in their interior. Such an experience is refreshing many by offering them an opportunity to confide more of themselves than is safe or practical at the office or even in the home or church.

While I have been appalled at some of the cruel bludgeoning participants have received in some "sensitivity sessions," in a warmly Christian atmosphere one small group can move mountains off individual shoulders. The prying mind can present obstacles to such a family circle; so can those who talk too much. But with a blessing, the ministry of friendly candor among a dozen people can perform wonders.

Let me tell you briefly about the experience of one small group which met for one week. Even the surroundings were conducive to reflection—beautiful stone buildings just below a spring-fed river, away from the fever of the city. About fifty of us met together for addresses on Scripture and personal relationships to begin the morning; afterward we met twice daily in circles of twelve. Throughout that week we kept the same seats. After the initial round of introducing ourselves, the leader began our first session by asking each person to name the animal he felt he most resembled or wished to emulate. I was a little surprised at so strange an opening, then amazed at how quickly that strategy melted our strangeness into a fellowship.

The leader began by introducing himself as something like a beaver. "I like to keep busy," he said, "and I don't think of myself as looking like much." All were animated and ready with their animals when their turns came. A fine looking young attorney responded, "I would like to be a male lion, for everyone is always making demands on me at the office and at home. I understand that the male lion eats and sleeps when he feels like it, and he doesn't even have to kill for it." An attractive young mother explained, "Frankly I envy the luxury of the housecat. She gets to be caressed and yet she keeps her composure. There is a part of herself she doesn't give away." Another woman volunteered that she still stood in awe of the uncomplaining gallantry with which her family's beloved black mare had met her death in foaling her little buckskin filly.

I am still amazed by the height and depth of the esprit de corps that was summoned so swiftly the very first day in that initial exchange. It made us immediately at home and expectant. That opener is not the only one. Each one can just as well be asked how he happened to get his middle or his nickname, or why he preferred the one he didn't get. Each one must name himself for the others in a way that is not pat, but that supplies a fresh clue to his true identity.

Such an authentic introduction prepared the way for the leader's second question: "Would you care to share an experience that stretched you recently?" There was no pressure. "You may say 'I pass' if you wish, with no loss of face and without losing your turn later if you want it."

The question immediately arose, "How much should one share of himself in such a situation?" The consensus was that he should say whatever he was meant to say to that group at that time. Each should say only what the setting and the company evoked from him. There is a danger both in under- and over-exposure. One should tell all to God, and it is often necessary to tell all to one's counselor or confessor in order to feel he has told it to God. While one should probably not tell the whole truth to a small group, he may share more of it than he can tell to everybody. St. Paul spoke of the thorn in his side, but he kept the nature of it to himself and to God, and perhaps to his beloved physician. That much candor might have been out of place in a small group, but there is so much that is in place there that should not come out in public.

One distinguished-looking man in his fifties jumped at the chance to begin the second round. "I'm a long way from New England, so I'll tell you what's tormenting me. My wife has become infatuated with a younger man." He shared the hurt and confusion over this unfair trick that had been

played on him, a poor innocent man, until it began to dawn
on him that perhaps he was not innocent. His colleagues
did not presume to advise him. They drew him out. As the
week drew to a close, this negative judge began to accept
blame for his tyranny in that home. He decided to go back
and do something about being a different person. He had
entered the small group haughty and indignant. He left disarmed, requesting, "Please give me a prayer for the road."

One woman cried, "I still go through the tortures of the
damned because of my former weight. I always stood out
so much larger than my classmates. On my first day in the
fourth grade the others encircled me with the taunt, 'There
stands Mount McKinley; there stands Mount McKinley.' "

At times when we met some were weeping before their
turn and before the words came. We found we were not
threatened. We experienced the love that "is not irritable
nor resentful." One young woman not yet married cried
about her parents: "They never once held me and told me
that they loved me." One brilliant and affluent man with the
utmost difficulty got out these words: "I never . . . before
this week saw the hurt in my wife's face . . . that I put
there." As the benediction of "Peace be with you" was
passed from hand to hand around the combined circles that
last night we met together, I couldn't help noticing that
same man receiving the blessing from his wife's handclasp
with tears glistening generously upon his cheeks.

Many times our honesty to God alone is what is called
for. On those huge occasions friends must wait in prayer in
the courtyard as Jesus asked his disciples while he went to
bare his soul alone. I am struck with the momentous consequences for hope in that confession.

I am not a Christian Scientist and am aware of the fantasy
that can so quickly imperil much faith healing. Nevertheless
I believe the story told me by a friend who is a Christian
Scientist. He is a Christian if I ever saw one, and he gave
me permission to use this story.

I have always enjoyed rugged health, but several years ago, I became acutely ill and began bleeding internally. I became convinced as I lay in bed that this was no passing ailment; I knew that I was near death. I was drawn with more pain than I could bear. I couldn't sleep. I could scarcely move nor get out of bed without help. Late one night with my last strength, I pulled myself to a sitting position beside my bed to make my peace with God. Several things that I had never made right in my life became very clear to me. I vowed to correct them if he would let me live. Suddenly while sitting there, I knew I had made my peace with God, and I was given the assurance then that I would be well. In a few days I was, and have been ever since.

There is the closest connection between honesty and health. Bracing companionship can bring us into our own. We can face what has happened and take the dare of identity. Friends hold up a mirror and open a window. Frankness then creates a field day for hope.

5
WISHING

Our hopes are not only based on honesty but are bound up with our ability to wish. Many wishes are wrong but wishing is necessary for the will to live. We must watch out for wishful thinking, but is there really any other kind? Freud found that every dream is in some way a wish fulfillment. Deep in the wishing well there is hope.

In some forms of mental illness the sufferer is unable to make any more wishes. He does not want anything for Christmas nor for his birthday. He does not want to go anywhere. He does not want to get up nor go to bed. His wishes never worked, so he won't allow himself to wish anymore. He has ceased to dream as far as he knows. A nightmare from which he wished escape would be a right step for him. He will never get well until he begins making wishes again.

It is often said of the American that all he wants is a little bit more. A young and ambitious politician was given an illuminated globe. He responded, "That is all I ever wanted." The donor observed, "Yes, the world." While the assignment of many of us lies in the direction of disciplining our wishes as with this man, for so many others it lies in distinguishing our own wishes from the other fellow's.

The Buddhist rejects all wishing. He is embarrassed by any lingering desire that he has not yet been able to eliminate. He is determined to bury the wishbone and be above it all. The curse he puts on wishing is philosophical, not violent. Christianity to the contrary wants the world but in the right way. The Christian's cry is, "O world, I cannot hold you close enough." The child wants his mother, the man wants a woman, a task, and passionately, its success. It is then in order for him to wish at last with Johann Sebastian Bach, "Come, sweet death."

What we are after from the inert is the recovery of their powers of wishing. We want the sick to get well enough to whisper, "Water," or "Kitty," or "Please love me, hold me."

Wishing may have a harder time outside the hospital. There are so many of us lost in the stuffing of the suburbs who haven't the slightest notion of what we would really like to do. We have obliviously substituted others' wishes for our own. There are many people who detest bridge, but who are playing bridge night after night because others have wished it on them. Their wishes are out of their control and they adopt them according to the commercials or because it's the thing to do. It is not that people want something and are being denied but rather that they do not know what they truly want.

A minister asked a couple in their forties if they would go as sponsors on a weekend camping trip with forty junior-high youths. The wife really wished to go, and the husband agreed to go as though it were a privilege. He actually would have preferred almost any other alternative for that weekend than going camping, but he never would have acknowledged himself to be a poor sport about church work.

Why was that man this way? He was brought up as a boy to do whatever was expected of him and to like it. He was

not allowed to have wishes unless they coincided with his
parents'. Wishing was wrong. It was selfish. He was made
to feel guilty for having normal sexual desires and for
having preferences which contradicted his mother's ideas
for his spare time. A child's wishes cannot be permitted to
reign unchecked, but this man's wishing apparatus had been
practically abolished, an extreme case of a very common
problem.

His childhood was scheduled as tightly at home as at
military school. His mother organized him, assumed his
wishes, and preempted his plans for Saturday night. She
read his mind and filled his plate. He played when he was
supposed to play with the toys "that that dear Dr. Gesell had
discovered were right for bright children in that stage of
development." When the time came, she put her idea of the
book that he would like in his hand, and at page twenty-five
she turned out the light and pecked him always in the same
spot on each cheek.

Mother knew best; how could he know what he wanted?
When he was asked a question, she answered for him. She
managed him through college until she met just the girl for
him. When he took his evening out, she tucked the money
in his pocket, put the part in his hair where heaven meant it
to go, held his favorite coat for him, put the words in his
mouth for the maître d'hôtel, and gaily sent him off.

His mother always went with him, even long after he had
a home of his own. Though she was dead and gone, she was
still there staring over his shoulder, peering down his throat,
counting his coughs, and picking out his socks. She continued to put words in his mouth and thoughts in his head.
His preferences were pushed aside into his unconscious
mind. Ever after when the church, club, or school alumni
spoke to him, he stood dutifully at attention and might just
as well have recited as before, "Coming, Mother."

That weekend with the young people became hell for him
because he hadn't the slightest notion why he was so un-

happy in the midst of everybody else's hilarity. He felt afraid to appear to be a party pooper, and he forced himself to laugh harder and stay up later. His redoubled effort, going against the grain of his true desires, doubled his anguish.

The poor fellow soon found himself loathing the youngsters and despising his wife for no satisfactory reason he could explain to himself. As penance he ran extra trips, served Cokes to all around him, solicitous as a robot programmed to be a boy scout. Unconsciously he was revolted by the hot dogs, but one is not supposed to dislike the all-American meat around a campfire where everyone else is noisily enjoying himself. So he sat in the circle with the rest, dutifully bolting down the hot dogs as they came by, sweating, smiling, and repeating to anyone who seemed suspicious of him, "What fun this is!" Inwardly he was scarcely able to contain the rebellion about to burst from his clenched teeth and up from his knotted stomach.

Can we find our way here between a Nero who does nothing out of regard for the wishes of others and the man whose own wishes are completely dissolved by the dominance of others?

A balanced example of what we are seeking is in someone such as Daniel Boone. It is difficult to meet the real Boone in the midst of so much television myth, but according to his authoritative biographers, Daniel Boone lived until he was eighty-five. Immediately after giving his age, one author added, "Boone always did what he pleased." I do not believe that this means that Boone was selfish, but rather that he did not feel guilty about doing what he wanted to do. This is loving one's self in the best sense of the word.

The Great Commandment orders us to love our neighbor *as ourself*, but we are never taught to keep the commandment that way. Loving our neighbor is preached at us, and we are made to feel guilty for self-love as though we are called on to apologize for our every new hat or car. Many do break the commandment to love their neighbor but more suffer from a lack of self-love. They become sick from a diet of nothing but self-denial and from concealing an accelerating accent on self-love.

Perhaps the chief reason why there is so little love of neighbor is that there is so little healthy love of self. If children were allowed to love themselves, to indulge their own wishes, to enjoy their thoughts and things because God commanded it, it would be so much easier to develop a genuinely spontaneous love of neighbor. The woman wearing a dazzling new dress has an easier time enjoying her neighbor's latest creation. The man with a fine car finds it possible to appreciate that twinkling sports job sitting in the drive across the street. The man who appreciates himself is prepared to appreciate his fellow-man.

Life is not this literal, but the only person who can enjoy his neighbor and, when the time comes, truly make a sacrifice of joy, is that one who was loved enough to love himself.

We love because God first loved us through someone else. Finally we become able to love others who cannot return our love. True love is filled with good wishes toward others. Loving is longing. This is why St. Augustine could honestly say to us, "Love Christ and do as you please." Out of the grace that comes from loving and being loved, one finds himself actually wishing others well, enough to work for them.

God is our meat and drink. We were all made to "hunger and thirst for righteousness." No matter who we are, "our souls are restless until they rest in Thee." Christ came not to stuff our wishes back down our throats but to coax them out right side up. "The thief comes with the sole intention of stealing and killing and destroying, but I came to bring them life, and far more life than before" (John 10:10, Phillips). Keeping Christ company matures our wishes until they match our hope, until our prayer is our passion to be free, to be forgiven, until Christmas to us means Christ's coming, until our faith burns with wishing, "Oh that I knew where I might find him!" (Job 23:3).

God listens when wishing attains that height. "If with all your heart ye truly seek me, ye shall ever surely find me." [1] To wish with hope takes waiting.

6
THE
ART
OF
WAITING

*It is now or never to the baby. The little child cannot under-*stand nor endure delay. Earth's education in postponement comes as a painful surprise, for at first we are full of wishes that won't wait. An infant has no past or future. All he knows is now. A sense of history and a memory of the future take time. The newcomer demands immediate satisfaction or becomes hysterical.

I have no intention of erasing the idea of hope for you. The time comes when our most seasoned veterans of delay need wait no longer. Extremities announce that hope is ready to pay off. It is proper to pray for our daily bread and absurd to consider God incapable of punctuality. He is usually waiting for us.

Yet life enlarges from the embryo only by slowing wishes down and by drawing blessings out as far as they will go. An instantaneous heaven could cancel creation's idea of time and space. To have all our hopes come true tonight would cause a tragic abortion. Christmas takes time and a sense of timing. The gifts of hope have to wait for us to grow up to them. Faith has ideas, love gets involved, and hope has to have time on its hands.

This is no excuse for the perpetuation of injustice. Those who have stood in line too long should demand their turn. The privileged cannot be too prompt in the removal of any obstacle to the underdog's fair share. While the now generation has much growing up to do, they deserve quick remedial service for having been shortchanged. Their parents spoiled them with things to get rid of them. Many of these unhappy and alienated young men and women could do as they pleased as long as they kept out from under foot. Others were tied down at home in a full nelson of emotional strings. Their exasperation flared to fill the vacuum. If they have been taught to get their way by tantrums, or if we have used discipline without devotion, we must take blame and corrective steps.

It would have been wrong to postpone the American Revolution or to delay the elopement of a couple who could not get out of their domestic prisons any other way. When others are standing on someone and won't get off, he must break away or die for not trying.

However, most of us Americans are not frozen to our seats but have worked ourselves into a lather of impatience. Even old people are exasperated with young people, widening the generation gap into a gulf. For years now cocktail parties have been restless places where everyone is shouting at once. Many salesmen have itchy feet and roving eyes, and the desks of old tycoons reverberate from drumming fingers and frantic calls from child brides. Senior citizens cannot sit still or retire; the life of the retirement village is frantically social. Many of the superannuated cannot relax to sleep or die without a pill, but are controlled by the reins of terror-reducing drugs.

It is no wonder that we wander into age so ill-prepared for the advanced assignment of reflection and leisure. Our way of life is not schooling us for serenity. We want instant service at the drive-in bank and the drive-in restaurant. Shortly at the drive-in funeral home one need not get out of his car to pay respects; the corpse is in the window display and three bars of Bach will play as you drive by.

The nation itself is so pushed it assumes speed to be progress. Faster cars, jets, and accelerated programs at school are considered improvements, but they may be merely symptoms of impatience. We want new homes, new cars, and new clothes immediately. We cannot wait until we can afford them, so we pay for them in installments and live now off next month's money. Americans on the average cannot keep the same address for longer than five years. Ministers who used to serve a church for a generation now bob about the country like itinerant frontier evangelists.

This speed-up winds our children tight. They cannot wait until Christmas to open their presents. They cannot wait until high school to date. They cannot wait to go steady, to live in co-ed dorms on campus, to have sexual relations before marriage, to get married, to have a child, to marry again and again. They are old long before their time because they cannot wait. No wonder the look in our time is so withered and young. Men and women have bolted life down but have not taken the time to digest it or to savor the blessings it would have borne had they the aplomb to pace themselves properly. "Joy is a fruit that Americans eat green." [2]

No sleepy little town is ideal, but before the junior chamber of commerce boosts any corporation who will bring business, why not ask what growth has done for New York

City? There ought to be something better for a city to look forward to than to become a boom town.

New York streets are paved with cars bumper to bumper; drivers are leaning on their horns and shouting things to each other that are not solving the problems of air pollution. Christmas rushes the entire year. No one pays any attention to anything except a crash program. The new Lincoln Center is fenced off and on by strikers and stacks of garbage. The customer cannot wait and the customer is always right; the town has gone berserk trying to meet its deadlines.

New York City is not the only one who cannot wait. Neither could I. I could not wait to get to college. Then when World War II broke out, I could not wait to leave my freshman year and enlist in the navy at eighteen. While others I envied were winning the war and covering themselves with glory, the navy gave me a lesson in waiting. At first I thought I was taking a beating in deferrals.

I had graduated from boot camp at Great Lakes and landed in the V-12 Officers' Training Program at Western Michigan. The twenty months of sedentary study looming ahead of me while my he-man boot camp buddies were already tasting the salt were more than I could stand. I made an appointment with the commandant of the post to put in a request for transfer to active duty as a seaman so I could see some action before the war was over and I was robbed of my place in the Hall of Fame. My eyes were riveted on the stars on his ribbons. I would one day realize that he was a great friend to me, but just then his brutal words hurt: "Redding, you are a damn fool. Stick to your studies. You'll be in the thick of it soon enough." I had been reassigned to *my* war. There is a time to fight and a time to cool one's heels.

Twenty months later it was graduation day at USNR Midshipman's School, Columbia University. Many of us had applied for PT boat duty, for they were the fastest ships afloat. We stood confidently at ease in the passageways of

John Jay Hall that day as our billets were broadcast over
the loudspeaker: "Ensign Redding, U.S.S. *Idaho.*" An old
World War I battleship. Slow. Out went glory with the PT
boat. I began to feel like the man in the symphony who
played the triangle; he kept holding up the thing to strike
his note, and the conductor kept hissing, "Not yet."

Since the whereabouts of each ship was top secret, I was
directed from New York City to the Bureau of Naval Infor-
mation in San Francisco to await further orders of trans-
portation. I traveled there by plane lest I keep the *Idaho*
waiting unnecessarily for me in the bay. I taxied from the
airport into the offices of the navy only to find that my trans-
portation had not arrived. I was one of the first in line early
each morning to be told that there was no word for me. I
played tennis for two weeks, convinced my records had been
lost and growing increasingly suspicious as to the extent of
heroism expected of me in the war effort. Finally my trans-
portation arrived. I hastened to the dock to be rushed to the
front. It was an old liberty ship converted to a baby aircraft
carrier. They wouldn't tell us where we were going, but we
were in the Pacific and the best she could do was about
eleven knots.

Thirty days later, bloated from our abuse of the shipment
of Nestle's chocolate aboard, we staggered ashore at Samar
in the Philippines. I promptly asked for directions to the
Idaho and was told that she had steamed off a week earlier
for Japanese waters. I was instructed to wait in Tent 24
until orders arrived for me. Twenty months of training, fifteen thousand miles, a month at sea, and the great-grand-
daddy of all PT boats had pulled away without me for what
I was sure would be the last round of the war.

It was. After taking atabrine and playing pitch and catch
for days on end in the Philippine sun with memorable nights
swatting mosquitoes, V-J Day came. How could I ever bear
to tell the neighbors? Some of us tried to hunt down one or
two unextinguished Japanese sharpshooters hiding in the

nearby hills, who kept pecking away at us as we watched the movies at night. It is a wonder we didn't scalp each other to have something to show for it.

Finally word came that the *Idaho* had been crippled by a Kamikaze that had hit her in the bridge in the final round of conflict, and she had headed for San Francisco where she expected to meet me. A freighter was waiting in the bay to take me to my battleship. Apparently my assignment was to bring the heroic crew of the *Idaho* congratulations from the transient officers' club.

We made better time on the return trip for we could sail direct now that the war was over. In twelve days we raised Hawaii, and after nearly capsizing in the sixty-foot waves of a typhoon on the old *Saratoga*, we made it under the golden gates of San Francisco—less than a month from the South Pacific.

I could not wait to inspect the damage on the *Idaho*. At least *my ship* had seen action. I was informed, however, that the *Idaho* had not docked in San Francisco after all. She had sailed directly for Newport Navy Yards via Panama. I was assigned to a troop train that used all the sidings out of respect for scheduled runs, and in a little over six days, traveling backward and forward day and night, I actually made it across the country with the veterans of World War II.

So after thirty thousand miles and more than three months later, just a few miles down the beach from where I had started out, I hurried up the gangplank of the wounded *Idaho* to render my salute and say the words that I had practiced around the world: "Ensign Redding reporting for duty, sir." The officer of the deck nonchalantly returned the salute and informed me that the officers had just been requested to gather on the afterdeck for a personal word from the captain.

Trying to look as though I had been aboard forever, I went aft and fell in line for what appeared to be a formal review. "Men," said the captain, a distinguished gray-haired Gary Cooper of a man, "I have just received orders to take command of another ship and will be leaving this afternoon. Most of you will be receiving orders of transfer in a day or two, leaving only a skeleton crew aboard. At this time I am going to pass among you and shake each of your hands in personal commendation for your gallantry that distinguished our old lady in action and brought her safely to her last resting place." The captain shook my hand fervently too as he went by. "Thank you, son." I said, "It was nothing."

I assisted a bosun's mate in putting one sixteen-inch gun to sleep and in sixty days received orders to report to U. S. N. G. H. Q. in Shanghai, China. Traveling at my usual rate of speed, two of us thirty nights later requested permission to board LST 122 tied up in Shanghai. It was late but we insisted upon announcing ourselves to the captain immediately.

We were white-gloved and in evening attire exactly as the officer's manual outlined. A gravelly voice came from inside the captain's cabin. Assuming it meant welcome, we entered at attention. The captain was sitting on the side of his bunk in his skivvies. He had not been shaving. He looked at us groggily, gestured vaguely in the direction of the half-emptied bottle of creme de menthe and fell over on the bed.

Such experiences taught me the true nature of the enemy and reoriented me to the kind of war in which I was to become actively engaged. We did work hard in school and there were fatiguing overtime periods of activity, but World War II to me was chiefly a course in waiting. That LST did permit me to salvage some of my self-respect, but I would not trade anything for the friendships, the humor, and the perspective that are forced to emerge when one realizes that life is making a fool out of him.

I do not mean to dampen the bravery of those who so well deserved their Purple Hearts. With all the sailors' yarns among shipmates as on the battlefield, uncommon valor was a common virtue. While men could deteriorate in the peacetime navy, dramatized so well in *Mr. Roberts*, inactivity can nurture another kind of heroism excavating in us a depth because we are not under fire. The navy tried to teach me how to knock it off. There is a stamina that can come only from standing watch.

The awful curse upon our heads is the curse of self-importance. As deflating as it is to be defeated in one's dreams and to be benched, it is in this reducing exercise that we have hopes of being freed of having to be famous.

The baby comes into the world king of the universe. Life best serves us by disengaging us from this treacherous illusion. Our hard knocks and preposterous delays may be necessary reminders that we are not Jesus Christ, not indispensable. The embarrassing meantime is God's way of upstaging us. God intends to stretch us out of our kingdom and into his. If necessary, he has to sock us out of his seat lest we die in self-deceit.

God did not create the world with a snap of his fingers. There were some controversial delays in those seven days to say the least, for "with the Lord one day is like a thousand years and a thousand years like one day" (2 Pet. 3:8, NEB). Whatever the fourth dimension is, it is interwoven with waiting.

Life is like gardening, baking, fishing, or learning to fly a plane. There is no way around the hours. Winter is a way of marinating us for more than we were ready for last April. What we call an accident may be nature's way of recuperating us from more than a fractured thigh bone.

Harvest time takes waiting as well as planting. Healthy waiting executes all the intermediate steps. Waiting is not stagnating. We do what we can and then we relax when it is someone else's turn. Sitting in the shade is a rich experience if the hoeing is done. We are not to do all or nothing. We are to adapt to our part.

Mingling our work with our waiting requires a delicate

balancing act. It not only takes time but a sense of timing to know when which is called for, action or rest. Life demands that we be sensitive and flexible enough to learn its rhythm. When does one pray? When does one put the legs on his prayers? We cultivate discernment by trial and error and by finding our way between the extremes of the eager beaver and the vegetating sloth.

Noble Penelope waited twenty years for her husband, Odysseus, to come home from the Trojan war. Her home was jammed for years with insistent suitors who thought her grief extreme. She delayed, to enjoy her hope that her lord and master was still living. Yet she realistically devised a strategy to meet the situation. She promised her avid wooers that she would marry one of them as soon as she finished weaving the garment she was working on. Each night, however, she unravelled what she had woven that day. It took a score of years but her beloved Odysseus did return, and her hoping across the years made that homecoming momentous enough for even Homer to remember. How did she know how long to wait? She knew. And yet she did not know. She followed the path that opened to her. Her investment returned to her "good measure pressed down, shaken and running over."

Waiting is a work of art. We will not be good waiters without a guide. George Washington wondered whether Valley Forge was worth all the frozen feet. How many feet would it take? Was the price of waiting worth it? Washington put his whole mind on it under God and was able to wait until just the right time. Edison tried out hundreds of worthless filaments to get his electric lamp to light. Bystanders believed him to be a mad scientist. They said he worked without sleep, but his discovery of the right filament was a triumph of a waiting, working combination. This patience was exemplified most beautifully by old Simeon who had longed for the consolation of Israel and who lived by the promise that "he should not see death, before he had seen the Lord's Christ" (Luke 2:26). It was not in vain. "Now Lord, let thy servant depart in peace for mine eyes have seen. . . ."

Jesus' disciples asked him to teach them to pray and he gave them the prayer that bears his name and which we have learned by heart. Perhaps his men tried it out and did not find quick relief. He gave them a second lesson in prayer. It had to do with waiting. "And he told them a parable, to the effect that they ought always to pray and not lose heart" (Luke 18:1, RSV). One story was about a man who finally got up at midnight to give a neighbor a loaf of bread just to get rid of him. Another was about a callous judge who cared for nobody but finally helped a widow for fear she would wear him out by her continually coming to him. It was Jesus' way of getting across to us that if even people opposed to helping us would help us if we kept at them, surely we can count on our Father coming to our rescue if we insist. "They that wait upon the Lord . . . shall mount up with wings . . ." (Isa. 40:31). He is worth waiting for.

Thanks be to God he does not give us exactly what we ask for at first! The interval often makes us realize that what we thought we wanted would have been the worst possible thing that could have happened. Or, as we continue to wrestle with the angel, we may discover that we don't need what we thought we did. Prayer and time together improve the picture we have and prepare us for a happier solution than we originally envisioned. We find our prayers changing into the right shape, for he is bending us to delight in his will.

Galileo made a pilgrimage to the tomb of St. Anthony, intent upon a boon from God. The journey was long and hard. It gave him time to think about the life and the sacrifice of this saint, whose blessing Galileo coveted. What a man he must have been to have given up so much for God! Anthony had surrendered the pride of position, his purse, the love of women and of a son. By the time Galileo had reached the tomb of that inspiring man, he too had become a different man and found himself praying an altogether different prayer than he had set out to make: "St. Anthony, intercede for me to Jesus Christ so that I too may do something great to serve mankind."

If we wait long enough we will find the shortest way home to him who has been waiting for us. In one way God's work is all done. He is the waiting Father watching out the window, listening for our footfall, ready to run out at any time and sweep any returning son into the arms of joy.

7

WHO
CARES?

Hope won't wait without love. These two are Siamese twins.
The good news won't keep and God himself cannot long
remain upright in anyone's eyes when one runs out of love.
Even the loveliest afterglow from our childhood grows dim
and cold if the bright circle of faces shining on us now
breaks up. Brilliant psychiatry washes off and shock treat-
ments only make more scars if no one really "gives a damn"
about what's-his-name who takes the prescription.

The kiss at the door, the touch on the covers that tucks
you in at night, or the handwritten letter lying on the table
in the hall prompt hope. If we don't tug at someone's heart-
strings we cannot face tomorrow. Hope not only takes timely
outside help at birth; it calls for the helpers themselves until
our last breath.

The Christian virtue of hope sticks out like a theological
sore thumb without the love that goes with it. When we
say love, we mean the love that is "patient and kind"; that
"alters not when it alteration finds"; that St. Paul further

defines in the thirteenth chapter of his First Letter to the
Corinthians. What Paul puts there in words must come to
life in us or we'll lose hope in words.

"You are not keeping house, you are burying it!" The
irate husband had given up hope and turned on his wife.
At first his wife had allowed the ironing, then the mending,
to get farther and farther ahead of her until it had become
a family eyesore. He had delivered repeated ultimatums,
then taken away her privileges, practically placing her under house arrest. To his utter consternation, instead of cor-
recting her this aggravated things further.

Stacks of laundry rose like skyscrapers from the dining
room table so that no meals could be served there for
months. Magazines and newspapers accumulated on the
dining room chairs and the living room sofa until guests had
difficulty finding a seat. The cleaning woman quit because
there were no longer any surfaces to dust. Finally, unsorted
boxes of things found their way along the window seats,
then flowed down on the floor along the wall and down one
side of the hallway. Violent scenes followed the times the
husband fell over these obstacles as he attempted to locate
the bathroom at night.

The husband clung grimly to the slim comfort he received from the rest of the family as well as from the neighborhood. All were taking his side. His wife stoutly refused
all offers of family assistance to help sort and organize. "I
know exactly where everything is!" He became embittered
but bore it nobly.

The housewife had lost hope too. Bad as her side appeared on the surface, she was not the only offender in that
house. Her incorrigible housekeeping was her way of
screaming at her husband, "You don't really love me!"

She was right. He had become so preoccupied with her
procrastination he could not see anything in her to appreciate. Since he saw himself as a martyr instead of as a party
to a quarrel, he made it a point to remember her birthday,

but his regard was regimented to official bounds which he set. He took no pleasure in her. He recoiled politely from her kiss. His spontaneous attentions had chilled into courtesies.

The relationship was undeclared war. When she dallied, he increased the pressure of his disapproval. She retaliated by letting things slip further and then he would cancel their vacation. Her messy house was her rolling pin. In return for her housebreaking she took an emotional beating from him. He refused to sleep with her. They were both conducting military operations and neither would admit it. As monstrous as one person may be in a marriage, there are always two or more sides.

She tried fitfully to bring order to the house, ignorant of the contradictory wishes welling up to block her. Instead of being cherished, she felt threatened. She was in a state of siege which so weakened and distracted her that she was unable to concentrate effectively on the job at hand. The domestic ground under her feet had been undermined by the denial of affection, and she was so absorbed unconsciously with that emergency that it consumed her energy and her powers of attention. She was literally burying the house her husband had broken by his abdication as her lover. The whole truth was too terrible to face so she numbly wore a veil of normalcy. In reality, her husband's exterior pose and his interior rejection had panicked her and rendered her useless and resentful. She took refuge in eating, dropped her make-up, and let her hair go. He made himself scarce.

Were they meant for each other? Yes. Was this wife acting in character? No. But would this husband die before being able to take the blame and give the love that would disarm the situation?

Their deterioration and the defensive poses that had frozen beyond the reach of a good talking-to had all resulted from a loss of the hope which collapsed for the lack of love.

A not-too-unusual bride and groom had collided. Instead of working things out constructively, they had lost confidence and were slugging it out. They hesitated to talk about problems. They proceeded immediately to war as people characteristically do under those circumstances, erecting higher and higher fences, carrying on demoralizing conversations and carrying murder in their hearts during the more incensed silences. So long as they were loveless it was hopeless.

A friend loved her way into the picture. She had loved them both and had avoided the pitfall of choosing sides and egging on the argument. They loved her enough to talk themselves out to her separately. She invited their confidence. Her understanding vented fury; it did not fan it. It was as though hope had to wait until an inclusive love broke through the pride of the husband. The resurrection of that home would be deferred until he had a change of heart. It was this larger love of their senior friend for them both that finally melted him. One day he came home from work and noticed a handkerchief stained red with his wife's blood. It was not just a nosebleed to him. It was his wife's blood, as though he had drawn it in his condescending swordplay. He found himself weeping, "I am sorry. Forgive me." Those are just words, but when they come from the heart, they go to the heart.

The tension thawed. War won't work if one side does an about-face. To disarm with love is to be truly disarming. When one stops picking up stones and begins gathering the flowers that are there and planting more, he is soon performing wonders of peace. Instead of trying to maneuver her into efficiency and reproaching her with reform, he turned on himself the criticism by which he had leveled her. This finally relaxed her fury of defensiveness. His was not the strategy of a weekend, but became a way of life. He had enlisted under another command.

Part of what he was up to now was a waiting game. He had already tasted the most delicious victory which was over himself. The progress now was not neat nor automatic, but he began whistling in the shower.

She was forced to reorient. The guns of the invading army had vanished. She did not need to wreck his house to get his attention. Unconsciously she had deeply needed the spontaneous expressions of affection which motivate good housekeeping. She set off some final volleys as make-up work and to make sure, but the daylight breaking in was more attractive than the dream world in which she had been hiding.

They had begun to minister to each other's needs instead of withholding them. He deeply needed the house in order to allow him to relax from the demands of his work, just as she deeply needed his expressions of devotion. "I get things done," she said later, "because he loves me unconditionally now whether or not I get things done." Her desire now was to please him whether or not he showered her with attentions.

Not everyone subjected to this superior treatment turns into herself on such short notice. A new woman is a work of God, not a husband's controlled experiment. We are not supposed to reform each other, but "to love and to cherish until death us do part." Yet when someone at last finds himself loving, anything can happen. Whatever happens will be far better than the hopeless way it went when love was dead.

Think of the national consequences of so personal a thing as love. We have referred to Washington's waiting at Valley Forge until it came time to strike. How much love it took to wait out the American Revolution! Freeman's award-winning writings on the life of Washington introduce one not simply to the man's endurance but to his extraordinary capacity for affection.

Exhaustive studies have convinced Freeman that there is not the slightest foundation for the scandals that small minds readily fasten on the father of our country. The man who was able to rule those scrapping colonies and the man they permitted to rule them could rule himself. Freeman astonishes the reader with Washington's *love* for his men, his country, and Martha.

The heroic hope it took to get us through that unavoidable war was born of the love, not exclusively the faith, of our fathers. At the farewell dinner Washington held for his officers, he signified that he would like to greet each one of them personally before they separated forever. The reception line formed to take Washington's hand. Henry Knox was the first to step forward. He had stood fast by Washington's side through the hell of waiting and bewilderment. More than any other he had trained the first American army into fighting shape. Suddenly Washington was overcome with emotion. He ignored Knox's outstretched hand and hugged him, weeping openly in front of his men. And so it went down the line. He embraced each man and wept for them all. When the war was over, Washington rode nonstop day and night to get home to Martha. If we wonder what it was that pulled this country together and held it, we could talk further about this man who cared enough about this place to be called its father.

What virtue characterized Sir Thomas More, Henry VIII's imprisoned chancellor? He stayed in the tower and would not bend to the king's will. What kept him in that grim isolation? That took great courage, a fine loyalty, a splendid honesty. Yet according to Robert Bolt, the "man for all seasons" was braced by that one cardinal virtue. More's daughter Margaret pleads, "But in reason! Haven't you done as much as God can reasonably want?" More replies, "Well, finally . . . it isn't a matter of reason. Finally, it's a matter of love." [1]

Our lost generation lacks the love that lasts. The best brains cannot be fully mobilized without love's ignition. A parent's heartlessness as well as heredity may account for a boy's apparently low IQ. We credit a mother's love for rearing the man whose intellectual contribution, more than any other, entitles him to be called "the Father of the Western World," Augustine.

Until he was in his thirties, Augustine's genius was spent on his own academic advancement and on devouring voraciously any girl caught in his web. He said in his confessions that he was seducing the women who were praying beside him in church. His mother, Monica, carried on a marathon of intercession. She besought the help of priest upon priest for her son. I believe her prayers matured her first until her mother's love permitted the love of God. She prayed the years down. The neighbors sadly smiled and shook their heads, for Augustine had won world renown as a professor and as a prodigal.

Monica made her way finally to the door of an old bishop. She wept prostrate at his feet and clutched at his robe. He stared down. It was about her son. At last the words came to him that he should say to her: "Go thy way and God bless thee, for it is not possible that the son of these tears should perish." [2]

As her body had once brought Augustine into the world, her love bore him into sainthood. He was sitting in a garden, he said, when it happened. His second birth was much more noticeable than the first, even to those who meet him now.

While others sat around lamenting the dreadful sack and fall of Rome, Augustine saw the period of waiting as a time of writing before the learning of the ancient world was lost forever in the dust. By the time he was finished with his shelf of classics, this father of the church had gathered into his volumes the library of Western thought up to that time and laid it at the feet of the new world—for the love of God. Martin Luther and John Calvin started the Reformation with those volumes of St. Augustine whose transformation resulted from a waiting mother's love. We turn now to her Primary Source.

III
THE
ORIGIN
OF
HOPE

8
OUR ONLY HOPE

"Our only hope," as the distinguished French Christian,
Desbuquois, has said, "is the love of God." God is hope's
hero. He is the reason wishing will not stop with mere hoping for this or that. It is he who has commanded us to hope
in him now and forever. He coined the word *to hope* and the
word is still warm from the touch of his hand.

Albert Camus and Jean Paul Sartre are absolutely right
to curse life if God is false. Their death of God has dashed
their hope, and hope soon flies away from anyone if he no
longer turns his face to God.

Seeing God only in the good the neighbors do is not
enough. Friends are only human and cannot always find us.
Our hope is anchored by a God with arms of his own who
can come and go on his own. I am not getting anthropo-
morphic. I am only getting personal with God. He is someone to love, someone who loves us.

Without God religion becomes a hopeless controversy to
kick around when we have time to kill. Without God there

for us the church meeting soon succumbs to simply massing for an attack on a project or a budget. If God is nothing more than a good word for the unknowable or a word we find ourselves misusing only when we get very tired, is it any wonder to us that hope is cheap? If we no longer know a God who can and will take care of himself and us we shall lose heart, for our Father in heaven was our only hope. The sad state of the world now is no excuse for us to lose this faith, for as C. S. Lewis has so forcefully stated, the goodness and greatness of God dawned on Boethius while he was waiting in prison to be beaten to death and on St. Augustine as he reflected on the fall and sack of Rome.

Imagine how hope would leap to its feet the very instant God moved back into our picture. If we should suddenly discover that God is, it would shake open our stale old theological cage. The eruption of God into our lives would slit those pat answers and pet questions we have slung at him ever since we were defiant sophomores. If we entertained for a minute the possibility that God is for real not even death could hold back the rush of expectations.

Hope was born from the encounter of a particular God and a particular man. It originated from a specific contract that God made with Abraham almost two thousand years before Christ. Abraham and God had such a close relationship that the Old Testament uses the same intimate word for a man to *know* God as it uses for a man to *know* a woman. Since hope entered history with this momentous relationship, we must mark it well.

Apparently pagan Abraham had had enough of his dreary obligations to an exasperating committee of overlapping little gods and the obnoxious pretense of profiting priests. This initial rendezvous took place in what has aptly been called "the cradle of civilization," the Fertile Crescent, in what certainly combined the London and New York of those days, the city of Ur. God spoke to Abraham in the same manner as he addresses listeners now. This was not an exchange that took place incidentally; it was a trial run, pioneering terrain that would become a familiar working definition across the future to all the faithful.

For all we know, Abraham grew suspicious that his boredom and restlessness were signs of this new God's way of inviting him to a better life. Having had all he could take of Ur's religious commercials, with nothing to lose but a life fast losing its meaning, he gambled everything that he was not hearing voices but a Voice which seemed to be inviting him to a territory to the west. At least he read his premonitions that way and went out, "not knowing where he was to go."

Abraham's unbelievable intercourse with God stimulated the Old Testament into writing, and this book would forever after attach the name of this man to the divinity he identified. We still pray to the God of Abraham. The book would not have materialized nor lasted if Abraham's dreams of descendants and a promised land had turned out to be a mirage. History swiftly tramples under the gods who cannot keep their promises. The Old Testament stands as a memorial that the bargain these two made was kept and is alive.

God was no longer an unknown quantity but was already leading Abraham to water holes before he was out of sight of Haran. What is so fascinating in the context of hope is that the name that Abraham gave to God was not El, "Thou art," as Jürgen Moltmann points out in his impressive *Theology of Hope*. "His name is a wayfaring name." [1] (Yhwh) This God that intercepted Abraham was not only a God who could get one out of town. He soon distinguished himself unforgettably as a traveling companion. Abraham was able to talk back to him and then make up with him again. Isaac, Jacob, and Joseph had similar experiences. Just as it had been foretold to Abraham in the days of his aged Sarah's barrenness, descendants fell like stars into his promised land. Stars are still falling into our promised land from Abraham's creating hope. Our journey is not over, but the course on which he was set led to Christ and still does.

That famous acquaintance between God and Abraham began the biography of a God who has continued to come through for men left choking in the dust of false gods. Men from Moses to David tested that hope with their lives and verified that it held good all the way to Egypt and back into downtown Jerusalem.

When their promised land ran out of corn, the clan was fed by one of their very own family direct from Pharaoh's palace. God had smuggled Joseph into Egypt as a blessing in disguise far ahead of time so he could have Egypt's granaries all packed for the famine God foresaw. When Egypt later turned on the Israelites in fury, they were released by plagues which Pharaoh believed Moses' God had sent. Finally, when they were chased by the grand army of the Nile until their backs were to the wall of waters of the Red Sea, a path opened to rescue only them. Later while the vultures circled overhead, manna came. Hope would feed on that fuel for a long, long time. The blessed memory of God's dramatic entrances sustained morale through rugged desert experiences and is recounted over and over throughout the Bible.

We are not hanging now simply by the thread of these ancient successes hope once enjoyed, but growing in the garden God has been hoeing by the hour ever since. God's thumb is as green and as graceful as ever. In the light of Abraham our rendezvous with God is ready.

Such an awesome beginning guarantees the ultimate coup d'état. Why do men object to such a pilgrimage? Because it is obsolete? Are we too sophisticated to take the superstitions of this legendary nomad seriously? No.

The reason men refuse the God of Abraham and retreat to a humanist position is moral rather than intellectual. We tell ourselves that our disbelief is based on scholarship. In reality we are using academic loopholes to excuse ourselves. We don't want to give God a chance because of the cost to our self-control. We think up every excuse we can to ditch God. We convince ourselves there are no sincere preachers and all godliness is pretense or naïveté. Our minds do not dictate our lives. Our minds are the willing slaves of our self-willed wishes and don't want any interference from the competition of God.

Do we know what still stands between us and God? Is it learning? No. Is it because we have come of age and have run God out of business? No. Is it because we have tried God out and he doesn't work? No. The obstacle between us and God is our will. We want our own way and we will stack the deck of facts to suit ourselves. God didn't have a chance among Abraham's friends back in Ur for the same reason. Like them we shuffle everything we know to best advantage. I may be misjudging others' rejection of God by the machinations of my own mind, but I have taken the negative side in too many bull sessions not to see that the secret reason we were damaging the idea of God was to get rid of him. Trying to disprove God is a form of running. Unless we can outwit him, we have to give ourselves up and face him. Tell yourself God is dead or he won't work, or do good on your own and then *you* can be God.

There is another slightly different objection to God which I would call an emotional block. The teen-ager who has had a raw deal in parents is going to have a hard time believing that the God who gave him those parents is any good either. He will project upon the cosmos the foul play that shook his baby buggy. Not having found love on the piece of earth where he awakened, he cannot believe that love is behind the rest of it. These young people have a lot of emotional unloading to do before they begin taking on a good God.

We are no more objective about God than we are about our mothers. Even when teaching the Bible strictly as literature at the university level I have noticed how swiftly it aroused the strongest feelings, positive and negative, among students who one would have assumed could not have cared less. One can never discuss God in an atmosphere of cold scientific inquiry. Any seminar on God is immediately embroiled or buried with emotions of guilt, hostility, and love, consciously or unconsciously. The atheist claims that the comments of the proponent of God are weighted with sentiment. His own comments are just as charged with negative feeling. Behind his accusations against God the Father is often the unspoken rancor, "You haven't met *my* father! I could have killed him! At least I will kill my father's God!" Not until he resolves these feelings can such a lad even permit anyone else in the universe to have faith in a Father.

There are those who claim that their repeated cries to God go unanswered. I know of those pitifully sick ones who are unable to cry out to God, but their tragedy lies in their not being able to get the door of their own heart open. God knows that their bottleneck is not their fault. For the rest, the revivalist may offer too pat an answer when he guarantees the magic of conversion within ninety days if one will only pray and read Scripture avidly in warm Christian company. The sales pitch, "Do this and you can't miss," may be a bit presumptuous or impetuous, yet I myself am embarrassed by the number for whom this works. Such a strategy may be over-simplified, and it may overlook the unique path which each pilgrim must take from the point where he alone comes, but it is basically correct.

There are those who apparently fall down their cliff and no juniper bush jumps out to grab them to safety. We cannot doubt the casualties cramming the hospitals and the files of the police department. The vegetable existence of the senile invites no neat solutions. However, talking about misery in general is a distraction. We will never find God in the abstract. We perceive him in specifics. If we appeal to him in a particular problem, God appears.

Rather than wasting time arguing over headlines, let us go to God and experiment. Ninety-nine men can arrive on an island and sit around in an advanced seminar of armchair philosophy and convince themselves beyond the shadow of a doubt that the island has never been inhabited by anyone else. Nonetheless if the one hundredth man finds larger tracks than any of them make, and if he finds evidence of campfires none of them built, the findings of that one research fellow are enough to destroy the most determined myth of all the rest. This one man can burn all the fingers of the disbelievers in the holy fires he has found.

This style of life insists that you are involved in a conversation with the same God that started talking to Abraham. Could what you wish for this moment, or the question that has been haunting you for the last few days, remind you of a "still small voice"?

For years the word *providence* to me meant only the capital of Rhode Island until John Baillie, that lovable old Scots theologian, showed me its import in his last lecture series in this country. He told how providence worked for him in his bridge game. He had been obsessed with bridge for years, thriving on its triumphs, richly entertained by the defeats of his faithful adversaries. Suddenly, for no reason he could find, he suffered a shocking losing streak. Soon it struck him that someone might be trying to tell him something. In fact, his losses burned him so badly that he was persuaded that this was God's way of graduating him from a sport that he had worshiped long enough.

Another's losing streak might mean that he should practice harder, get some rest, or go back and learn how to take a licking. Each must ask what his own dilemma means to him. God is up to something in our lives. He shows his hand between the lines of our daily activities. Our dented fenders and sore throats may combine to chorus that we should slow down. The unexpected bonus at the office breathes with meaning in the light of those dreams we have been having, those calls we have been getting. How else but by the way life was hitting him do you suppose Hamlet was led to his conclusion: "There's a divinity that shapes our ends, rough hew them how we will"?

God is not simply broadcasting general principles in the Scripture or on Sunday morning. He speaks directly to us and in detail, and it may be the very opposite of the sermon another hears. For some reason our mind fastens on one word and goes off with it in a direction no one else takes. This may be God's word to us. How many tragedies could have been averted if we had only read the handwriting on our wall or attended to the feeling in our bones on time. Earth is no stray planet adrift from God's world. Neither are we. We are not out of his magnetic field. If he is sovereign over the huge network of finely jewelled galaxies, then he has attended meticulously to each detail to make the whole work out beautifully. A proper orbit demands precision to the millionth of an inch or second as do our landings on the moon.

Our private world is not off bounds to God. "There is not a word in my tongue, but, lo, O Lord, Thou knowest it altogether" (Ps. 139:4). God is much too modern and the requirements of creation too exacting for him to have left anything miscellaneous. For him "the very hairs of your head are all numbered" (Matt. 10:30) and "Are not two sparrows sold for a farthing? and one of them shall not fall on the ground without your Father" (Matt. 10:29). He left nothing to chance in snowflakes and atoms, no Tiny Tim omitted from the temper of his art.

Abraham was accustomed to capricious gods whose main interest in men, when it existed, was only with huge multitudes. This God took time out from the army to talk to Abraham privately.

I am one of the reluctant ones who has come to trust what has been hard for me to call Holy Writ. Even the words have become holy to me now and I find them ringing true. The words of an illustrious commentator do not possess the sacramental force of such words as, "Moses, Moses . . . put off thy shoes from off thy feet for the place whereon thou standest is holy ground" (Exod. 3:5). Or as the voice addressed a lad: "Samuel, Samuel." The little boy that night knew he heard a voice and kept running to old Eli to see what he wanted. Old Eli kept telling him, "I didn't call, go back to bed." Finally it occurred to the old priest as the boy kept coming to his bedside in the night so resolutely that someone else was calling him. And Eli said, "Go, lie down and it shall be, if he call thee, that thou shalt say, Speak, Lord, for thy servant heareth" (1 Sam. 3:9).

We make religion complicated and easy. It is not. It is simple and hard. We do know more about God now, but they knew him. We are better students, but they were better off, existentially. Our discovery of hygiene has not eliminated our need for bread. God is still our only hope. "Today if ye will hear his voice, Harden not your heart" (Ps. 95:7b,8a).

9
THE
GROUND
OF
HOPE

God is our only hope, but we must have more convincing grounds for it than Moses' burning bush and Abraham's water holes. Fastening hope so that nothing can remove it will require even more than God's fingerprints. All of his personal touches in the lives of those around us reassure, but it is not enough. In order for hope to endure the brutality of life it must have massive foundations.

Hope cannot be perpetuated through commandments. It can last only so long on promises. It soon shrivels into wishful thinking without a miracle.

We have it. Our best Man rose from the dead much improved physically. Before each reader makes up his mind the same old way about this heroic surgery, let us first appreciate one undisputed fact. The word *gospel* comes from the words *good news*, and this good news burst from a grave that had been opened from the inside.

Easter was all there was to Christianity at first. It was this cemetery scandal that sent men scouring the countryside for further details of the life of Christ. Because of the incredible whirlwind tour of a murdered man, they compiled his Sermon on the Mount and preserved his parables. Without his return they would not have bothered to recover his remarks. All the memories that we have of him, the Lord's Prayer, even Christmas itself, are not Christmas presents but are ours because of Easter. The resurrection built us a hope chest of everything he said and did.

Facts and friends quickly collected around this Easter story and its weekly celebration until there was enough volatile material to make the Bible over and enough heroism to suffer the birth pangs of a church. Mysteriously there is enough hope left over from this occasion not only to make a heaven for us but to give us an appetite for it.

No one has ever cast any lasting suspicion over Christ's existence and execution. There was a time when enough of a stir was raised about whether he really ever lived to shock Voltaire, but history soon laid the controversy to rest in Christ's favor as it had when the Gnostics challenged his incarnation. The most skeptical historian no longer doubts that Jesus at least lived and died.

Confidence in Easter, however, has collapsed among the majority of contemporary Christians, an attitude which has knocked hope senseless. One of the ways by which we may recapture the impact of Easter is to return to the scene of the crime. Let me conduct you on a brief tour of that tomb from which hope gushed with such artesian force that it accounts for whatever hope we have had since. Easter was not intended to be an added burden to our incredulity but rather God's sublime concession to our suspicious natures.

A mob of curiosity seekers gathered on a hill outside Jerusalem to watch the agony of a young carpenter's last gasps for breath. He was dying between two thieves. The three were sagging from spikes pounded through their cartilage into huge wooden crosses. They were stretched up there that afternoon for all to see what happened to those who dared to defy the rulers of the Romans and the Jews. No doubt a few noticed the Roman soldier shove the long spear into the carpenter's stomach from below and push it upward as far as it could go. The big man on the end of it never knew. He was already gone. It was just to make sure. Blood gushed out on the upright and all over on the ground below him. We are told these hard things by those who were telling on themselves, and perhaps it is not so strange that scenes from that day might stick in their minds with deadly accuracy.

After that the sun went out and the mob took off in all directions on a sudden rampage of terror. They did not run for their lives that night but for their souls. It was hysteria born of the blood on their hands; as the darkness swallowed them we are told they were beating their breasts. It was a day that would take longer than a lifetime to live down.

Later that night two men of great influence and considerable means in the capital risked everything to ask Pilate for the body. Nicodemus and Joseph of Arimathea lent what distinction and valor there was to a night that was otherwise unrelieved from ignominy. Rembrandt put them there in our minds forever by catching them at work on their scaffolding, getting him down. There they are, with tear-streaked and ashen faces, tenderly unfastening his arms, lovingly trying to atone for the avalanche of shame that had fallen on the world after it was too late, and he was finished.

The women who had loved him watched them to the bitter end wrestle the already stiffened form into a beautiful tomb which, apparently, Joseph had been saving for himself. He then saw to it that a huge stone was rolled across the door of the tomb and departed. Pilate ordered guards posted who sealed the stone and stood watch against any threat of the disciples stealing the body.

They need not have feared. That Friday's business had been sufficient to devastate the last tremors of what could be called a following. Jesus' second in command had been busy for hours disavowing any connection, and before night fell, grief had gouged out the last eyes of any hope in Christ. They had no more heart left in them for anything. The tomb was safe from them. If any disciples could have been found, I doubt if they could have been whipped into that graveyard then.

No one needed to remind them that Christianity was through. They were still hemorrhaging so badly from the gashes Good Friday hacked in them that they could not bear to have anyone touch the subject of the coming of the Messiah. It would not be easy to get their hopes up ever again. They would not be sticking their necks out anymore, thank you.

Early Sunday morning while it was still dark, Mary Magdalene, Mary the mother of James, and Joanna (Luke 24:10, NEB) could not bear to stay away any longer. They knew there was no way to get in to him, yet they had scraped together a handful of sweet-smelling herbs and finally found themselves at the graveyard.

According to John, Magdalene was the first to discover that the tomb had been plundered. No other alternative occurred to her. Horrified by this final indignity, she flew to break the bad news to the disciples. "They have taken the Lord out of his tomb" (John 20:2, NEB). Peter and John ran all the way back and verified her findings. The corpse had been unwrapped and hauled off.

Like Mary, Peter and John never suspected any other possibility than vandalism. John underscores this: "Until then they had not understood the scriptures, which showed that he must rise from the dead" (John 20:9, NEB). Despite all of Jesus' advance notices that death could not hold him, his death had driven his hope out of their minds. Perhaps the disciples seemed naïvely overconfident about Christ before the crucifixion, but afterward no atheist could have surpassed their skepticism.

Not even the women were expecting Easter that weekend.

All were there to show respect for the dead and to embalm
a body. They were only too well aware of how well he had
been crossed out forever. Nothing could have been more
remote from their minds than that he had gotten up off his
slab and walked out. Mary Magdalene represents our modern cynicism, for instead of her suggesting so outlandish a
thing as Jesus being alive she was sanely wringing her
hands and soberly racking her brain as to what could have
become of his poor battered and decaying flesh.

This was Pilate's reaction. The Jews bribed the soldiers
to spread the word that the body had been stolen. The bribe
was an unnecessary precaution, for most archaeologists of
the Holy Land to this day believe without being paid that his
body was stolen. Most scholars are already inclined to regret
the absence of his body in the grave just as the disciples did.

Year after year across the land the great majority of us
are taking Easter substantially as John notes the disciples
were taking it on their first trip to the tomb. They peeked in
the tomb and went home. Go to church the Sunday after
Easter and see for yourself how seriously men take Easter.
Almost no one believes it and I have been one of them. If
men believed, they would be back in larger numbers immediately after Easter for more than they have been getting in
church. Usually they are not back and they are not expecting.

No one really objects to this much Easter but no one will
believe another word of what we are told happened next
without something conspicuous happening to him. To form
another opinion about the Resurrection involves a change of
heart. The obstacle to one's belief in Easter may not be the
lack of evidence for it but inside resistance to the idea of
having to face God under the glaring light of the next world.
Our verdict about the Resurrection is only partly a matter
of intelligence. It is also a moral question.

Something in Mary Magdalene made her search the tomb
the second time, and by this time there was an angel at the

head and one at the foot of where he had been. She was so busy looking for the dead among the living that their appearance made absolutely no impression upon her. Then she turned to speak to the gardener who had at last arrived, and she vented her frustration on him: "If it is you, sir, who removed him, tell me where you have laid him, and I will take him away" (John 20:15, NEB). An overturned tomb, two angels added, and the hauntingly familiar face of the gardener had not even distracted Mary's funeral mind. She is the first to whom God wished to unveil his master stroke.

Then the gardener broke the spell of despair by saying her name, "Mary," and that gave Christ away to her again: "Master."

When she found her voice and found the disciples, she said the word that until very recently I have only read: "I have seen the Lord!" (John 20:18, NEB). They had not seen him so the words meant nothing more to them than they had to Mary before he had happened to her. And their words seemed to them as idle tales, and they believed them not (Luke 24:11). We ourselves could not have formed a more effective society for the prevention of the Resurrection than we possessed in that disillusioned committee of conscientious objectors, who also dismissed their informants as hysterical women.

This idle tale had gone far enough! Their hearts were not only broken, their reputation was ruined. They had not only been wrong; Christ had made fools of them. He had suffered but he had escaped, leaving them holding this preposterous bag and the mess to clean up. This clever April Fool had not been made in secret Nazareth but in front of everybody.

Feelings such as this must have compounded the grief of the disciples. Otherwise I cannot account for their rude refusals of a resurrection he had solemnly promised them so often before. Their procrastination was not only due to heartbreak and mental strain but also to bitter disillusionment.

No enemy of Christ could have scorned the report of his
resurrection any more obnoxiously than Thomas: "Unless I
see in his own hands the mark of the nails, and put my finger where the nails were, and put my hand into his side, I
will never believe!" (John 20:25, Phillips). If a more con-
temptuous blasphemy has ever been uttered, I have never
heard it. This is no doubting but rather a damning Thomas.
The case was not only closed, it was smeared. Apparently
Pilate was not the only one who had washed his hands of
that business, although, by comparison, his controlled reaction appears contrite.

No ghosts in the garden nor the hallucinations of women
whom pain had pushed too far could have broken the deadlock of disbelief. The risen Jesus would have to be made of
something more substantial than a silhouette against the
morning sun or a fancy that struck the unstable. If he died
like a lamb, he would have to roar his return like a lion or
be overlooked.

That is practically what he did. He forced his way
through their doors and on their attention. They could not
get away. The idea that the sweet spirit of Jesus drifted
back to massage old memories in the somber aftermath of
the Upper Room is all imagination. Jesus stormed the room!
Mark states that he "reproached them for their incredulity
and dullness, because they had not believed those who had
seen him risen from the dead" (Mark 16:14, NEB). The
force of his personality and the fact that death had made
him hungry practically frightened them to death. "Have you
anything here to eat?" (Luke 24:41, NEB). He would not
permit them to shelve him in heavenly shadows. He was not
only not diminished; he had undergone bewildering improvement. He was more real than they were. "Look at my
hands and feet. It is I myself. Touch me and see; no ghost
has flesh and bones as you can see that I have" (Luke 24:39,
NEB). They might not remember that they were in the
Upper Room, but they would never forget that Jesus was

there. He was not there simply in spirit. There was more
of him there than at the Last Supper.

Jesus did not whisper to Peter to give Thomas his regards
when Thomas finally came around. Christ broke up that
meeting, among other things, to get Thomas. Some of us
have been allowed to persist in our treason. Thomas was
cornered. It says "the doors were locked" (John 20:26,
NEB). Thomas had asked for it and he was going to get
it so it would never come out. Jesus was enraged. He would
no longer put up with doubting Thomas. It is a wonder that
Thomas survived such evidence. What happened was at
least enough to kill doubting Thomas. "Reach your finger
here: see my hands; reach your hand *here* and put it *into*
my side . . . *believe!*" (John 20:27, NEB). "My Lord
. . . my God!" (John 20:28, NEB). "Because thou hast
seen me, thou hast believed: blessed are they that have not
seen, and yet have believed" (John 20:29). Here is the
solid and holy ground of hope.

SEVEN STANZAS AT EASTER
by John Updike

Make no mistake: if He rose at all
it was as His body;
if the cells' dissolution did not reverse, the
    molecules reknit, the amino acids rekindle
the Church will fall . . .

It was not as the flowers,
each soft Spring recurrent;
it was not as His Spirit in the mouths and fuddled
    eyes of the eleven apostles;
it was as His flesh: ours.

The same hinged thumbs and toes,
the same valved heart
that—pierced—dies, withered, decayed and then
    regathered out of His Father's might,
new strength to enclose.

Let us not mock God with metaphor,
analogy, sidestepping transcendence;
making of the event a parable, a sign painted in the
    faded credulity of earlier ages:
let us walk through the door.

The stone is rolled back, not papier-mache,
not a stone in a story,
but the vast rock of materiality that in the slow
    grinding of time will eclipse for each of us
the wide light of day.

And if we will have an angel at the tomb,
make it a real angel,
weighty with Max Planck's quanta, vivid with hair, opaque in
    the dawn light, robed in a real linen spun on a definite loom.

Let us not seek to make it less monstrous,
for our own convenience, our own sense of beauty,
lest, awakened in one unthinkable hour, we are embarrassed
    by the miracle,
and crushed by remonstrance. *

    * Reprinted by permission from HIS, student magazine of Inter-
Varsity Christian Fellowship, © 1964.

IV

HE
PROMISED

10

HEAVEN'S ALREADY HERE

Christ's resurrection has a hygienic effect immediately upon acceptance. In a sense a man goes to heaven as soon as he reads his name upon its waiting list. Heaven promptly advances installments of her bounty to the man who makes her his trust, just as one suffers far ahead of time with one foot in the hell he believes is coming to him.

The future we anticipate has an enormous effect upon us en route. If one assumes he will die like a dog one day, it damns him to dog days in the meantime. Entertaining the idea of ultimate oblivion contaminates the peace of mind one could otherwise have enjoyed tonight; and if one can entertain prospects of paradise seriously, it will enhance even his gravest difficulties.

The future we foresee for ourselves also has a way of magnetizing us to that end. It is folly to pretend that we can shrug death off as irrelevant. Consciously or unconsciously we are fascinated with the horror or the awe of this most demanding occasion confronting us. It is as though we tend

to throw ourselves in the direction of the way we think the
road goes. We attract the evidence to which we are inclined
which makes us even more inclined. We are bent or braced,
suited and shaped according to our approach. As we collect
confirmation to prove the wisdom of our vision, it collects us.

As Immanuel Kant observed, we really want our predic-
tions to come true. Therefore we look at everything in that
light and it returns that look. In this way, as Gabriel Marcel
has said, "Far from foreseeing my own destiny, I shall have
precipitated it." [1]

The voice on the other end of the telephone was calm.
"Your husband is going to be killed on his way home from
work tonight." The housewife shook so violently she could
not hang up the phone. She collapsed. The news of death's
approach disorganized her. Nothing had happened to her
husband. What undid her was the threat. While that sentence was never carried out, it took months for her to recover
from the brutality of that warning.

Such an incident illustrates the slow torture into which
one is initiated when it hits him that he too must die. You
and I are walking barometers of this weather forecast. Our
temperatures and blood pressures react. We are not going
to be much good for anything until we get it settled. We
may be able to conceal our bad news better than that wife
battered by the telephone threat, but if we believe that death
is the coming thing, we are going to get a taste of it along
the way. A man becomes more and more preoccupied by
his premonitions.

Paul Tillich has defined anxiety as "the state in which a
being is aware of its possible non-being." Despite our age's
billion dollar entertainment industry, Americans have no
more overcome the paralyzing terror of this last enemy
than the stricken victims of the bubonic plague. We may
conceal our terror better, but that only makes the situation
worse. The effects of a bad ending are "pocketed in ad-

vance." Tennessee Williams was brutally frank about this
in his introduction to *The Rose Tattoo:*

> Whether or not we admit it to ourselves, we are all haunted
> by a truly awful sense of impermanence. I have always had
> a particularly keen sense of this at New York cocktail parties,
> and that is perhaps why I drink the martinis almost as fast
> as I can snatch them from the tray . . . the moment after
> the phone has been hung up, the hand reaches for the scratch
> pad and scrawls the notation: 'Funeral Tuesday at five,
> Church of the Holy Redeemer, don't forget to send flowers.'
> And the same hand is only a little shakier than usual as it
> reaches some minutes later, for a highball glass that will
> pour a stupefaction over the kindled nerves. Fear and eva-
> sion are the two little beasts that chase each other's tails in
> the revolving wirecage of our nervous world. They distract
> us from feeling too much about things. Time rushes toward
> us with its hospital tray of infinitely varied narcotics, even
> while it is preparing us for its inevitably fatal operation.[2]

Our present time is not produced exclusively by a bache-
lor past. The future may be even more influential, for she
has the last word. Emily Dickinson always thanked her
first.

> The stimulus beyond the grave
> His countenance to see
> Supports me like imperial drams
> Afforded day by day.[3]

One cannot take love seriously without taking it eternally.
Any love that is applied as a temporary arrangement is a
form of puppy love. Christian love is unalterable and timeless. Anyone who stands by a grave and sighs, "I do not
believe in the next world," is unwittingly confessing in the
same breath that little love was lost on the one he buries
there. His love was not large enough to require a heaven to
hold it. Where there is love for someone, there will be irrepressible hope for that person too. A person who really
loves will find himself psychologically incapable of hope-

lessness. Only the person who is in love can appreciate how God feels about him. "For God so *loved* the world that he gave his only Son, that whoever believes in him should not perish but have eternal life" (John 3:16, RSV).

To conclude that the departed cannot live on except at the mercy of our absent-minded memory damns them to cramped quarters indeed. Whatever else could be said of such a dim view, it is certainly expecting too much of our yellowing photograph albums. The best that can be said of graveyard dismissal is that it is arrogant. It is as though an earthling refused the absentee any further enjoyment in a world superior to this. Skepticism represents an objection to any improvement in the dead man's affairs. When we say "How could God do this to her?" we are saying that we feel the life we have to offer her is better than anything God could offer. But belief in heaven robs the mourners of that half-conscious smugness that they have come off better in the exchange. Gilbert K. Chesterton exposed the heartlessness behind disbelief in the next world. "To be complacent about the prospect of [another's] extinction spells baseness and disloyalty." [4]

And so Gabriel Marcel, the French poet-philosopher, concludes, "There is no human love worthy of the name which does not represent for him who exercises it, both a pledge and a seed of immortality . . . to love a being is to say 'you, you in particular will never die.' " [5]

Hope in eternity flames from Easter. The New Testament grew out of that international incident which changed everything. Paul asserts, "If Christ was not raised then neither our preaching nor your faith has any meaning at all. . . . if the dead do not rise . . . and if Christ did not rise your faith is futile and your sins have never been forgiven. Moreover those who have died believing in Christ are utterly dead and gone. Truly, if our hope in Christ were limited to this life only we should, of all mankind, be the most to be pitied!" (1 Cor. 15:13–19, Phillips).

We must acknowledge, however, that the Resurrection and the next world to which it directs us is of interest only to those in love with God. The risen Christ was never seen by anyone who did not care to see him. All of the five hundred or so who ran into him after the Resurrection were believers. You will never find a Herod or a Caiaphas enjoying Easter.

One must be loved into the life that is more than life. Belief in heaven is not a conclusion we reach but a depth we touch. Without love the new creation stays in a textbook. Academically God is a good word for the unknown, and we are only cartons of nuts for the cosmic machine. Only love opens eyes to see that God has created man to be, not to be dead. It takes love to read between the lines of suffering and to know that he did not snap earth into a flash of consciousness simply to see if he could do it. Only loveless minds can depress geography into a grisly museum with a mushrooming collection of skulls. The man who has been loved recognizes the God of the living, not the God of the dead. Creation constructed loving room.

Those contemporaries of ours who have recklessly chewed off the climax of our creed did not know any better. "The resurrection of the body" is ridiculous if one reads it out of the context of "God the Father Almighty." If one's contact with God is limited to the classroom or to an unhappy childhood, he has never had enough love to believe that "God so loved the world." Only a loved one can even imagine a heavenly Father giving our bodies back to us in better condition than they arrived on earth.

Unless we enjoy God's company, our entire life and thought will be spent pulling in the horns of a faith that will seem to us to have been terribly exaggerated. The initiated, on the contrary, will be busy raising ceilings: "Eye hath not seen, nor ear heard, neither have entered into the heart of man, the things which God hath prepared for them that love him" (1 Cor. 2:9).

I am a father. I make many mistakes. My love is not all it should be, but my children know that I would do anything in my power for them. Think what you would do for yours. Do we think we would do better than God the Father for his? Our best only hints at his extravagance. Can we bear a God who can outstrip us parents?

Love knows this well enough to insist that the New Testament's comments on the characteristics of the life-to-come are no exaggeration. The risen Christ was larger than life as we know it here. The next world is not a letdown. Lovelessness depreciates the next world. It populates clouds with wan phantoms flitting by, strumming on cardboard harps. It is the most boring burlesque imaginable. That kind of ridicule is a caricature of the mansion to which the vastly improved Jesus introduced his men in the Upper Room.

Jesus was better off after death, for the resulting Resurrection enriched him beyond our imagining. The disciples were not seeing things. He could see things they couldn't see. They were the ghosts. They were the aging shadows of decomposing flesh. He had arrived. If he could get their hopes up to it, they could begin savoring the breathtaking reverberations: "Because I live, you too will live" (John 14:19, NEB).

We keep losing the precious distinctions in the life to come that Christ's reappearances guaranteed. If life here is meaningless, we have no wish for more. So many do not have the heart for hanging on to any more immortality than Plato admitted. The brilliance of the testament's climax keeps fading into irrelevant footnotes for the uninitiated. However the irreducible faith is there as soon as a man has heart to bear that much hope.

The heavenly man is no dim relative of his earthly self. His risen self is no remote descendant but developed in permanent color for which his former self on earth was the fragile negative. His brain will not be damaged nor will his memory suffer for it. The risen Jesus insisted, "It is I myself" (Luke 24:39, RSV).

But perhaps someone will ask: 'How is the resurrection achieved? With what sort of body do the dead arrive?' Now that is talking without using your minds! In your own experience you know that a seed does not germinate without itself 'dying.' When you sow a seed you do not sow the 'body' that will eventually be produced, but bare grain, of wheat, for example, or one of the other seeds. God gives the seed a 'body' according to his laws—a different 'body' to each kind of seed.

There are illustrations here of the raising of the dead. The body is 'sown' in corruption; but it is raised beyond the reach of corruption. It is 'sown' in dishonor; it is raised in splendor. It is sown in weakness; it is raised in power. It is sown a natural body; it is raised a spiritual body. As there is a natural body so will there be a spiritual body (1 Cor. 15:35–38; 42–44, Phillips).

Thank God the church does not weary us with celestial slides and tape recordings, but the veterans of his love appreciate Paul's preference for heaven over earth: "My desire is to depart and be with Christ" (Phil. 1:23, RSV). Anyone who feels sorry for a dead Christian, as though the poor chap were missing something, is himself missing the transfiguring promotion involved. This is what we mean by the good news. The place to be, the perfect place to build and settle down, is on the rise there following the last breath. "Be thou faithful unto death, and I will give thee a crown of life" (Rev. 2:10). "When I was a child, I spake as a child, I understood as a child, I thought as a child: but when I became a man, I put away childish things. For now we see through a glass, darkly; but then face to face: now I know in part; but then I shall know even as also I am known" (1 Cor. 13:11,12).

Experiencing this love proves what is coming. Mary Magdalene was not meeting a complete stranger in the garden. Easter dawned on an old friend. Believing in him after he died was possible because she had lived with him before. That companionship put death in its place. C. S. Lewis testified after the death of a friend, "When the thought of Charles Williams and the thought of death came together

in my mind, it was the thought of death that was changed."
An extraordinary soldier was obliterated by an exploding
shell. His stunned buddy found himself shouting, "It will
take more than that to stop him!"

The evidence for the life to come does not rest solely on
the integrity of those who told us that the tomb was empty.
What persuades us now is the love that this life cannot hold,
none the less real for being rare. "You yourselves are our
testimonial, written in your hearts and yet open for anyone
to inspect and read. You are an open letter about Christ
which we ourselves have written, not with pen and ink but
with the Spirit of the living God. Our message has been
engraved, not in stone but in living men and women" (2
Cor. 3:2–5, Phillips).

Eternal life does not wait for the deathbed to begin; it
begins whenever we give our hearts to God. Earth is meant
to be a maternity wing for both of our births, of the lungs
first and then of the heart. "The great Easter truth," according to Phillips Brooks, "is not that we are to live newly
after death—that is not the great thing—but that we are to
be new here and now by the power of the resurrection." [6]
Although a radical metamorphosis certainly does take place
upon death, we are really raised from the dead the day we
become attached to Christ.

Then what are we waiting for? Penitence. Easter's bright
and warming light is under eclipse for so many because they
have never said "I am sorry." Each person must come to the
place where he takes the blame. Each man deserves an experience of sin and pardon. Conversion is not a neat little
conference with God that tidily wraps up everything in an
afternoon. Yet the time when God proposes to a man and
is accepted overshadows any other engagement. Everyone
knows whether or not he has had such a honeymoon. The
experience of forgiveness occupies the minds of those so
honored.

So many professing Christians have never known love.

A woman would often rather bear to her grave unresolved grievances against her father than come out and admit that she did not come from a good home. It is quite an accomplishment to acknowledge that one was unloved. In this way millions of adults have sealed off their early years. It is the way to honor one's poor dead parents. It is thought that reporting the real situation would be poor sportsmanship. Many of us prefer to love our parents superficially than truly to forgive them. Couples carry on a continuing front of a loving marriage, but in actuality the feelings of wife and husband in their second home are often dictated by the real feelings that are still festering from the first. What the bride and groom have in a few years is not a love match but a repeat performance of their tragic childhood.

Being blind to their emotional malnutrition, they are blind to heaven's possibilities. When one bears a load of rancor for having been shortchanged and cannot allow himself to acknowledge it, it cuts him out of the early revenues of eternal life. He not only wants no more life after this but he has his hands full trying to last this life out. The idea of more life to come is repugnant. Such a neurotic Christian has had all the life he wants.

But when someone cares enough to hear out the bottled reserve of bitterness, a person can be reconciled for this fresh start. Armed with this insight into and freedom from the past, he is prepared for the plunge into his second birth and its beckoning future. With the old score settled, it is his turn to take responsibility for his sin.

Rembrandt, when he came to paint the scene of the crucifixion, penitently painted his own face into the mob. "Were you there when they crucified my Lord?" When this question finally makes one's flesh crawl for his own blows in the death of God, then he will cry for mercy enough to get it. The resulting new look is in such contrast to one's former perspective that it gives him something specific with which to encourage others. Penitence means that, like the publican, one cannot so much as lift his eyes to heaven: "God, be merciful to me a sinner."

Good Friday and Easter go together. A resurrection to righteousness is senseless unless one is dead in sin. Heaven is hidden by guilt. When we rise from our knees forgiven, we see heaven. The deadlock in this theological controversy is not broken by an academic conquest but in a very personal matter. The stone is rolled away from the tomb of our hearts when the pardon for our part in Good Friday concretely comes.

All this does not mean that death and temptation are cosily dismissed as soon as we fall at the feet of Christ. The going gets rough in the home stretch. No one can ever lightly say "I have arrived" or "I am saved." It would be better judgment to leave that verdict in the hands of him whom we proclaim to be the hope of the world. However, no one can ever know what it is to be forgiven without having visions as did John of Patmos: "I saw a new heaven and a new earth: for the first heaven and the first earth were passed away; and there was no more sea . . . Behold, I make all things new" (Rev 21:1, 5).

This vision is advanced to us in practical down-to-earth payments. Some will sing about their good health, for they have read life as saying, "Your faith has made you well" (Matt. 9:22, RSV). Others will rejoice in a friend they have found who held them fast "in sickness and in health, for better or for worse." The manna is versatile. One man delights in his forgiveness and another in the mystery of his success. But while the good news was still very young, the Master of it was able to report, "Seek first his kingdom . . . and all these things shall be yours as well" (Matt. 6:33, RSV).

11

A
DAY
AHEAD

Hope is a latecomer. Most of the march of time was made without hope. To the ancients, events drifted like dead leaves into the murky whirlpool of history. With the exception of Plato and Socrates, the Greeks assumed the worst was yet to come. Hope was a superstition. Everybody stoically braced himself to meet certain disaster. ". . . remember," Paul reminded his new congregation at Ephesus, "that at one time you Gentiles . . . were . . . separated from Christ, . . . having no hope . . ." (Eph. 2:11, 12, RSV).

The pagan Greeks were taught to despise hope as "the food of exiles," to use the words of Aeschylus. Euripides condemned hope as "man's curse." Hellenic schoolboys customarily memorized these words of Sophocles so they would never forget.

> Not to be born is past all prizing best,
> But when a man has seen the light, this
> Is next by far, that with all speed he
> Should go hither, whence he hath come.

While the serenity and reflective nature of Buddhism have so much to commend it, it is basically a religion obsessed with hopelessness. The object of Buddhism is to reach Nirvana by the Noble Eight-fold Path which means to kill every desire. Nirvana in the Sanskrit literally means "extinguished."

The religions of the Magi and the Hebrews are the only two places in the dark pages of the past illuminated by promise of a future with any lasting improvements. The novelty of their hope distinguishes them from all other religions save the three they inspired: Mithraism from the one, and Christianity and Islam from the other.

The Hebrews became convinced that history was not hysterical but sanely headed somewhere. A few of them finally got up their nerve to contradict the cynic, Ecclesiastes: there was too going to be something new under the sun. The act of creation itself promised consummation. As the old, old story unfolded, it fed this imagination until a prophet made a powerful suggestion. Isaiah broke the silence of night several centuries before Christmas:

> For behold, I create new heavens and a new earth; and the former things shall not be remembered or come into mind. The wolf and the lamb shall feed together, the lion shall eat straw like the ox; and dust shall be the serpent's food. They shall not hurt or destroy in all my holy mountain, says the Lord (Isa. 65:17, 25, RSV). . . . nation shall not lift up sword against nation, neither shall they learn war any more . . . (2:4b, RSV). The wolf shall dwell with the lamb, and the leopard shall lie down with the kid . . . and a little child shall lead them . . . for the earth shall be full of the knowledge of the Lord as the waters cover the sea (11:6,9, RSV).

Christianity is convinced that much of what Isaiah also foresaw about the Messiah has already occurred, as advertised in the new calendar which dated everything before and after the year of our Lord's birth.

God's lover's quarrel with the world is not over, but it has reached the mop-up stage. Noted New Testament scholar Oscar Cullman explains, "The church is now living in the time between the decisive battle and victory day." Since Christ won the decisive battle on the cross, we can be sure the war for the Kingdom is won. It is clear from the headlines that the ending is surely going to be a photofinish, requiring of us every conceivable heroism up to the last minute. Not yet in heaven, we still live and work in hope.

However, any expectation of Christ's return has been practically pressed out of the picture presented now in the papers or in the public school textbook. We have been brainwashed of the hope that Christ is going to stage a comeback. John the Baptist would jar New York City now as he did Jerusalem then. Churches that celebrate Bethlehem are embarrassed by Armageddon.

Any hope of God's bringing back his Kingdom was damned long ago by Renaissance optimism. Men took a fancy to arranging the future to suit themselves. For two hundred years we have been reassuring each other that every day in every way we are raising Utopia all by ourselves; why pray to God, "Thy Kingdom come"?

This perverted faith in human progress has pushed God off his throne and disinherited everyone who has worked so hard in the past by transferring all benefits to that lucky race of supermen waiting at the summit. Swallowing this idea of material progress means sharing substantially in the same long-range plans the Communists have in mind. It is an arrogant concept, that of rubbing God completely out of the picture, never permitting him to return.

However, two world wars have made the very idea of man-managed progress ridiculous. Such a childish philosophy doesn't fit the nuclear facts. We wonder if radioactivity will leave any posterity to which to leave our pollution. If each of us dies like a flower, won't the entire garden of humanity itself perish?

Science is nervous over several large gaps in her own

theory of evolution. Few scientists will now entertain that position without awkward reservations. This is not to deny Darwin's inestimable contribution but to be scientific enough to acknowledge that the whole story of man's biological trek is still a question. Our largest chunks of learning expose larger unknown quantities. The archaeologist is reluctant to concede progress over the centuries. The most he will admit is that man has acquired increasing control over his physical environment, although in the larger sense that too may be an illusion. Competing nations cancel one another's achievements. Every fresh stride in science can kick us back.

"Great modern artists, like Roger Fry, admire cave paintings not as curiosities, but as masterpieces," says John Baillie in *The Idea of Progress*.[1] Where are the successors to such saints as Francis of Assisi or Augustine? Why do we refer to our great religious leaders as reformers unless we imply they return us to a superior state existing in the past? So far we have failed to improve upon da Vinci, Michelangelo, Plato, Shakespeare, or the Bible.

While we do not recommend a return to the days of bloodletting and diphtheria, the idea that we have come of age must be chastened. All of the examples our age displays as proof of civilization's advance might prove to be a falling backward. Gutenberg's new printing press printed the Bible; ours have added the Communist Manifesto and pornography. Did the discovery of dynamite deserve the Nobel prize that it received? The marvelous mariner's compass has led its share of pirates, Nazis, and Kamikaze pilots. Has the film industry made a vital contribution to our pilgrimage to the eternal city? What does the airplane make you think of, hijackers, holidays, or bombers? We shall always have to hang our heads in shame that atomic energy made its debut at Hiroshima instead of at the World's Fair. Concentration camps are not the malicious crimes of ancient times which we've outgrown, but far more massive atrocities than Nebuchadnezzar had the capacity to administer. The cannibal chieftain cut through our illusions of superiority when he asked the American soldier in North Africa, "Why do you kill so many more people than you can eat?"

Technological refinements may not mean progress. If we survive this century and clang greedily into the next round with even heavier horseshoes hidden inside our boxing gloves, where will that get us except nearer hell? We can set up snappy zip code mail service to the moon and back, add a summer place on the south side of Venus, and yet remain where Byrd and Magellan left us. What is the advantage of stretching life as long as Methuselah, or mixing up men by the batch in our own clever little laboratories, if this only multiplies the agony and the absurdity? Who said the Pilgrims had it so much harder back there on Plymouth Rock? Before we start pitying them, we should ask if Christ would weep over Jerusalem if he saw it now.

The report of the death of God is true, but it is a case of mistaken identity. The corpse belongs to the god of progress. With that body out of the way, could we not be better prepared to believe in the return of the living God? It has always been difficult for men to believe that God could finish what he started. Scholars pity the apostles' passion for Christ's quick comeback. The joke may be on the scholars instead.

I do not mean to burlesque the Second Coming by packing suitcases for his prompt arrival at midnight tonight. I refer to an unscheduled hope free of such uninspired technicalities—an alert which could animate our humdrum habits. The typical Christian today acts as though God were only a swear word. The God of the apostles was athletic, quickwitted. God has not aged. Nor have we outgrown him. He is up to something surpassing our expectations, dependable but unpredictable. He is a God who has warned that he will return like a thief in the night.

The population explosion, the horror of atomic war, and the frenzy of our inventions carry a note of finality never felt before. The ominous environmental crisis and the rush of weird perversions remind us of a forgotten threat to vanity. Our last hope must no longer be forbidden territory. Eschatology is a burning issue. Marcel identifies what is in the air now as "the flavor of evensong."

We do not address each other stoically as those who are about to die en masse. The mounting pressure is not from approaching death but a deadline for transfiguration. It is not our funeral that is pushing us, but the more frightening marriage of heaven and earth. We are not to tidy up like the condemned, but to get dressed for the return of a Bridegroom. This huge adjustment does not distract us from everyday; it highlights it. We live as though each day mattered, every move counted, and as though God were not going to take forever.

We must not be so anxious to be delivered of the apostles' misconceptions of "when" that we miss their wisdom. Their God was moving near. The apostles' religion never put them to sleep; it drew them to the edge of their seats and made the landscape of experience alive with impending surprise.

The imminence of Christ's return cannot be misused as an excuse to get out of work. Have you ever watched a crew of sailors when a white glove inspection was due? Even the slackers heave to then. It is the hopelessness of having no God around that distracts us from duty. It is dread and despair that make us so anxious we cannot concentrate. Being responsible to someone brought the apostles a security that enabled them to keep their minds on their work. Though almost all of them died young, that tiny group of men accomplished more than all the war, legislation, and labor since.

Hope thrives on the suspense of God's next visit, whether or not it is his last. What would it do to the reign of monotony if suddenly we had a premonition that our time had come? That expectancy would send us flying to our posts.

"But who may abide the day of his coming? and who shall stand when he appeareth?" (Mal. 3:2).

We have been amused for so long by our forefathers' addiction to pie in the sky, but we are stuck playing in our mud pies. God has a more balanced diet in mind. And we can taste the first fruits.

The life that is literally expecting to see the face of God soon is inhabited by the hope a pregnant woman feels in the kick of her unborn child. We have watched the Kingdom coming within us in down payments of wonder and laughter. "Some of you standing here will not see death until you see the Lord come" (Matt. 16:28). This is the word of God. Sir John Seely in *Ecce Homo* spoke of the mysterious way this vast invasion is taking place:

> No man saw the building of the New Jerusalem, the workmen crowded together, the unfinished walls and unpaved streets, no man heard the clink of trowel and pick axe; it descended silently out of heaven from God.[2]

V

HOPE
DOES NOT
DISAPPOINT
US

12
THE
SENSE
OF
WONDER

Thornton Wilder throws open wide the door to wonder. His Emily in *Our Town* missed most of life's thrill too her first time through. After death she was granted special permission to go back and relive her twelfth birthday in Grovers' Corners. Her experience was a breathtaking entrance into the land of enchantment most of us never know about until it is too late.

Visiting her childhood once more made Emily cry, "There's Mr. Morgan's drug store. And there's the High School, forever and ever and ever. I can't look at everything hard enough." Wonder means allowing life to kiss you unexpectedly. While the rest are putting in time, the wonderers are lapping it up like Emily: "I can't look at everything hard enough." Wonder is hope's most delightful child.

Our Town not only puts life on its toes for a surprise ending, it also uncovers the birthdays we forgot to celebrate in the everydays. At least that sweet Emily reminded me that I forgot, along with almost everyone else, to light candles and blow them out on my bread as well as my cake.

How many acid sophomores sock life and its wonders with contempt. "Nothing ever happens around here." Those are the famous last words of shallow men who know nothing worth knowing. Those words were repeated one dreary afternoon in New Concord, Ohio, while astronaut-to-be Johnny Glenn was banging away on an old motor he had dragged from the junk yard. The provincial see nothing special in crossroads that roll up the sidewalks at seven.

"Catch any news down at the store, Ezra?" "Nope, nothin' 'ceptin' a new baby over at Tom Lincoln's."

"How did the revival services go last night, Ian?" "A poor showing it was, too. No one was converted save wee Davy Livingstone."

"Mrs. Franklin, don't tell me you are expecting your fifteenth?" "Yes, and if it's a boy, I'm going to name him Benjamin."

"No one in there but George, a Negro fiddlin' with chemicals." "George who?" "George Washington Carver."

The grindstone grinds up wonder. Workhorses have too many things to do to be bothered by the nonsense of stillness. Amahl, the crippled boy in Gian-Carlo Menotti's exquisite Christmas opera, *Amahl and the Night Visitors*, limps indoors shrieking with the ecstasy of the holy night, "Oh, Mother, come and see . . ." This poverty-stricken mother's despair had so accustomed her to expect the worst that she was trapped.

> Amahl:
> Oh, Mother, you should go out and see!
> There's never been such a sky!
> Damp clouds have shined it
> And soft winds have swept it
> As if to make ready for a King's ball,
> All its lanterns are lit,
> All its torches are burning,
> And its dark floor

Is shining like crystal.
Hanging over our roof
There is a star as large as a window,
And the star has a tail,
And it moves across the sky
Like a chariot on fire.

The Mother (wearily):
Oh! Amahl, when will you stop telling lies?
All day long you wander about in a dream.
Here we are with nothing to eat,
Not a stick of wood on the fire,
Not a drop of oil in the jug,
And all you do is worry your mother
With fairy tales.[1]

Wonder will die, according to our efficiency experts in Aldous Huxley's *Brave New World*. Babies can no longer be left to the mystery of birth in a modern technological state. *Mother* will become a dirty word. Scientifically controlled progeny will be picked off racks in supermarkets and conceived in sterile hatchery test tubes according to carefully prearranged specifications so that uncorking day will not be left in any doubt. We will have no more birthdays. We will celebrate the day we were decanted. What the embryo turns out to be—sex, hair, and eyes, height and IQ—will be tightly controlled by injection and conditioning. We won't have to worry about troublesome individual variations with these programmed personalities.

Carrying out "the year of our Ford" to its logical conclusion will mean being unable to tolerate any more unclassifiable nonsense by Shakespeare or to waste any time wondering about why we are here. Creation will be stuck, the wonder of life atrophied forever.

Wonder suffocates under all our things. The gold rush drowns sunsets in its dust and dries up the poetry of the wilderness. This passion for more poisons peace and puts gifts up for grabs. The rat race can't let a man catch his breath of miracle.

Sticklers for statistics are not free to entertain God's unexpected guests. Keeping one's trophies dusted and the crab
grass down can whittle away at one's finer hours. There is
nothing wrong with a man's owning private property, but
it is wrong for private property to own a man. The owner
can lose the luxuries of the summer, and sacrifice all rights
and benefits of songbirds and sunsets to the gardener and
the cook.

Wealthy Abraham and Joseph of Arimathea were just as
godly as poor St. Francis. But the Nazarene who had nothing
but the robe on his back and the sandals on his feet no doubt
enjoyed a liberty to wonder free from the accumulation of
goods that can hump our backs like camels. This does not
excuse those who have from feeding the have-nots, but is to
remind us all that man shall not live by bread *alone*.

Wonder has had millions mocking her long before the
Israelites began murmuring against Moses. "Pharaoh will
never let us go. If he does, there is the greedy Red Sea
all ready to gulp us down. If we survive it, those cannibal-
istic Canaanites will fry us for breakfast. Life is rigged
against us."

If God did die on the cross for our sakes, he gets no
thanks from us. God sent his Son—what do you say when
somebody does something kind? Some swore, "He is a
blasphemer who should be stoned." Others smiled and turned
away. They still do.

Others labeled him a maniac or subversive. Strangers
have damned him with faint smiles as a small-town saint as
his neighbors did: "Can anything good come out of Nazareth?" (John 1:46, RSV). They never bothered to answer
anything but long-distance calls and so despised a Savior-
in-residence.

The successors of these cynics now occupy some of our
most comfortable chairs of religion. "Jesus was," some say
in reluctant theological tones, "a teacher such as Socrates,
and the miracles made up about him must be myths." To

the blind, he is shrunk to a subject that needs to be treated instead of a master to be served.

Many lifetimes are consumed registering mild complaints against their lives. Robert Louis Stevenson flung himself in life's favor, taking death in his stride: "Gladly did I live and gladly die."

We are not meant to live led around by whatever carrot dangles on a stick, but to live at an altitude of wonder, working in a job that was made for us, not one for which we were made. We are not to be a cipher of someone else's success, but to come out as ourselves. G. K. Chesterton claims that wonder will spring two surprises on us. "First, that this world is a wild and startling place, which might have been quite different, but which is quite delightful; second, that before the wildness and delight one may well be modest and submit to the queerest limitations of so queer a kindness." [2]

Jesus was brutally frank about this doorway to wonder. It takes some doing: ". . . Whosoever shall not receive the kingdom of God as a little child, he shall not enter therein" (Mark 10:15). The shell of convention, the hell of congealing habits, our pride and prejudice, must be cracked.

The eyes of a child open wide with wonder. Not even a tadpole can get past him without a thorough examination. We say, "It's only a toad." The child says, "Let me hold it. Will I get warts? Where do toads come from?" Wonder will not take anything for granted. "Do they lay eggs? What does he eat? Can I keep him? See him blink! Did you see him snag that fly? A foot away and he never budged!"

Just because someone has stopped collecting toads doesn't mean he has exhausted the wonder in nature. Jainists in India may not be so eccentric, religiously sweeping the ants from underfoot. Reverence for life held Albert Schweitzer spellbound at the microscope before so despicable a speck as the tubercular bacillus.

Do you remember what it was that brought some of the

most profound poetry from Robert Burns? It was a louse;
and next, "that cowerin' beastie," a mouse. And Shakespeare
himself, in *As You Like It*, takes the child's toad to tell us
the meaning of human suffering:

> Sweet are the uses of adversity;
> Which, like the toad, ugly and venomous,
> Wears yet a precious jewel in his head.
> And this our life, exempt from public haunt,
> Finds tongues in trees, books in the running brooks,
> Sermons in stones, and good in everything.
> I would not change it.
> Amiens:
> Happy is your Grace,
> That can translate the stubbornness of fortune
> Into so quiet and so sweet a style.[3]

The pedantic man despises mud; the child makes mud
pies. The impressionable, happy child will make a morning's
worth of magic from an incident of spilled beans that the
man under the influence of self-importance would regard as
an irritating intrusion. Twenty-twenty vision isn't sufficient;
even being an expert at bird identification misses the mark.
There's more to see. Emily Dickinson saw past the oriole
in order to describe it so unforgettably as "One of the ones
that Midas touched." [4] Wonder walks on tiptoe, ready for
anything. To a child anything can happen, and only a child
of God has ears to hear: Nothing is impossible. Nothing—
even these mountains.

If we dare to suspect that God is alive, burning bushes
become possibilities in our own back yard. We would not be
able to recite, without a catch in the throat, "This nation
under God" in the pledge of allegiance. Looking back over
the harrowing days of bitter dispute and black despair
through which our infant nation finally bobbed to birth,
George Mason had seen enough to speak in awe. "It
seemed," he said, "as though we had been treading on en-
chanted ground." [5] This approach rescues entire continents

of experience from what is otherwise a graveyard in the making. If God has a good eye for detail and holds each of us dear to his heart, what is so fanciful about St. Francis taking the cardinal flashing into his view not as an accident but as God's deft brush-stroke perfectly timed to take his breath away?

Perhaps the joke is on us instead of on poor Job. Job insisted it was worth losing everything in order to find everything. Surely after all that heartbreak, he was not faking when he cried, "I have heard of thee by the hearing of the ear: but now mine eye seeth thee" (Job 42:5). Something strange got into that gallant battler for life, Robert Louis Stevenson, to make him dare to say, "I believe, and though I woke in hell, would still believe."

I have always had the most difficult time comprehending the Virgin Birth. I have also been increasingly disappointed by men who take the wonder out of it so they can manage it instead of having it hang precariously over our heads. Yet that story meant something unspeakably powerful to the children of astonishment, the apostles. As Will Durant has said so beautifully, for them "the story of the Virgin Birth was the masterpiece of understatement."

When will we think of the Bible as something to wonder over instead of to plot? Why must we nail everything down to some cross we can wear around our necks? Would it not be an act of intelligence to sit loose before the largesse in which we find ourselves and leave God a little working space, just in case? The more I think about it, the more impressed I become with Joseph the carpenter's confidence that his betrothed was actually pregnant by the Holy Ghost. What husband would believe the angel that informed him of so unlikely a story about his expectant bride? Any way we regard the story, we will be astonished. Where will that story, or the story behind it, or the story ever after take us? I have heard little children singing the spiritual, "Angels watching over *me*."

Emily exclaims at the close of her return to childhood in *Our Town*, "Do any human beings ever realize life while they live it—every, every minute?" What do you say? Life finally made Job gasp in amazement, "Things too wonderful for me!" (Job 42:3). It was death itself that prompted Hamlet to tell his faithful friend, "There are more things in heaven and earth, Horatio, than are dreamt of in your philosophy." Perhaps it is not too late for you and me to fall in love with this good life, until we too could find ourselves saying with Shakespeare's young lovers in *As You Like It*, "Wonderful, wonderful and most wonderful, and yet again, wonderful."

13
THE IMPOSSIBLE ALWAYS HAPPENS

Hope is the passion for the impossible. This faith engages us in the madness of loving the least deserving persons and in hoping for the most unlikely miracles. If love is a fool for loving her enemy, hope is a fool for expecting such love to work.

You can always count on water coming out of rock. That is the way creation works. Life on earth promises that life-giving rivers will flow in the deep ruts worn in our desolate society. Hope is not wanton nor naïve, but it obliges us to ask for what cannot be merely in a man's world, yet ought to be. Hope demands the contrary of the seemingly hard cold facts. This stone pushing down upon my heart was made to be rolled away. Your drouth was designed to be temporary. Man is not simply a subject for idle scientific speculation. Every tomb is suspect.

The cynic preaches the absurdity of any room for improvement. He has dismissed the world as impossible. Yet a seed of hope will move a mountain out of the way.

One of the mountains on the back of ministers today is the church herself. My father was one minister who left the church as a younger man. He had had an offer to play professional baseball, then had attended a Methodist revival and received a call to preach. He went into it with everything he had and became a Methodist circuit rider to twelve churches in the mountains. Fifteen years later he ran into what he called "higher criticism" and having a keen if unlettered mind, he lost confidence in the homespun biblical faith by which he had found his way into the ministry. He had also become sick of the phoniness that poisoned Protestantism, so he quit. I was a teen-ager, and I applauded. I knew I would never be a minister. We farmed together, loved it, and laughed behind the backs of the holy little preachers and holier church ladies whom mother invited to the house.

My aunt used to send me for Christmas what I assumed was the selection of the Book-of-the-Month Club that meant least to her that year. I was taking graduate work in English at a university and came home for the holidays to find that my Christmas present from her was *Out Of My Life and Thought* by Albert Schweitzer. I stayed up Christmas night reading it. That book shook me into seminary and upset my father's skepticism. We selected the most liberal school of theology so I would not go into this thing blindly as he had done.

When I think of impossible situations, I think of the predicament into which I fell when I left that seminary and landed in the pulpit of a church. It is no wonder to me that established ministers are backing out. I do not mean to condemn the fine church in which I found myself not long after graduation; I am rather confessing my own pilgrimage. I thought that I was a go-getter, but I tried everything to get that church going with not a hint of success. I painstakingly scheduled special evenings on controversial issues, and as I grew desperate, signed petitions for social action on the side.

I did succeed in raising a little stir between the church's left and right wings. That was all. I raced into the fall from each summer with a fresh crash program that crashed. The first night in Lent came, over which I had labored long and hard, and only six people showed up to get the word I had to give on the Book of Acts. Six.

I gave up and had my feet propped on my desk. At that point I was persuaded that there was far more hope for hardened convicts than for unmentionable Presbyterians. My father was right. The church was a burnt-out case.

Through the window of my study I saw John, a striking athletic-looking man, striding toward my door. I recognized him as one of the top executives of a large corporation, although only in his thirties. He had been a successful professional tennis player. He was one of those men who seem to win at whatever they set out to do and this man had made a million. I scarcely knew him. Why did he wish to see me?

Not in my wildest dreams could I have guessed what his first words to me would be. It had occurred to me as we shook hands that he and I were probably the closest friends of a doctor named Tony who had just suffered a terrible personal tragedy. "Dave," John said, "I feel that you and I are called to bring Tony to Christ." I was stunned. No one, before or since, has ever faced me with so forthright a directive. And for such a man as he was to say it left me paralyzed. Such a statement was considered bad form in my seminary. It was the very thing my father was trying to live down and I to avoid. I couldn't reply to this man that his proposal was none of my business. Yet whatever my business was, it had not been going too well.

As soon as I recovered from the shock, John and I got on famously, and I agreed to accompany him to see Tony. As the professional, I promised to tell Tony my reserved version of John's idea: "Tony, we feel that your recent tragedy may have placed some distance between you and God."

That evening a cornered Tony replied, "I know I am not perfect, but I don't think I'm that bad." Before the evening was over, it began to occur to me that there just might be a personal God after all, one with a sense of humor. Of the three men, I began to suspect that it was I, the minister, who had placed the greatest distance between himself and God. Before we left that night, John proposed we three meet Monday evenings for supper to see where it might lead. Having nothing better to do, I agreed.

We had fun eating together for a half hour, remembering Christ did too. Then we stayed quiet together for another half hour to see if anything would happen. It was virgin territory to me, but I was as weary as they were of pushing sterile programs and mustering endless committee meetings.

We had the time of our lives together. We began being ourselves. We let God be spontaneous instead of reviewing him cut and dried. Soon there were six of us. Six. Someone was prompted to suggest we go on a retreat together. John objected, "I have had a stomach-full of those cozy little prayer circles. Nothing doing unless we are going on one where we are going to be scared." That stopped us for a moment. Then we laid plans. Naturally we had to bring in a retreat leader from a great distance. We phoned one west of the Mississippi. "Will you come—for six men?" His speech slowed, "That's the smallest retreat I've ever led . . . but I'll come." Tony promised to take care of the provisions and the rest of us prepared for the impossible.

The keynote scripture reading at the retreat that night had to do with the rich young ruler, and to our astonishment he had come to the retreat. He was our sixth man, thanks to John. We will name him Mac. Late that night, stumbling about in the huge campground occupied by six men, one of us almost fell over a prostrate form, face down, hands outstretched, praying. It was John.

Yet attractive, engaging Mac almost stole the story of that retreat. He was a young man in his early thirties. He was from New England, well-nourished on private schools, and in his late twenties he had inherited the family toy firm which was slightly in the red but still functioning. Several years previously he had been operated on for a malignancy in the lung and appeared to be a terminal case. His athletic health came back instead, better than ever. It occurred to him that God had done it, but he could not bear to have any part in what he had seen of the church, so he became a Buddhist; much to his wife's dismay, he stared into flames and took the lotus position when he came home from work at night.

Next, he had noticed his small daughter playing one evening with a common household product. He modified it and marketed it so successfully he became a multi-millionaire practically overnight. Instead of patting himself on the back, he had the strongest impression that this again was the work of God. He became an expert in Buddhism and mingled it with his superb sense of humor. He signed one of his letters to me during the wave of Buddhist monks burning themselves to crisps of protest across the seas, "Warmest personal regards, the only Buddhist afraid of fire."

The effect of the retreat on Mac was not dampened by time. He came up to me one day months later: "Dave, I have become a Christian." Those are just words, but they carried weight with me that day because of the way Mac said them.

A few months later, I received a long distance phone call from Mac. "Dave, sit down. I'm calling from the New York Toy Fair. I feel called to go into the ministry." I soon recovered from shock and began to swell with pride about my part in landing this exciting fish. Mac, sensing my depravity immediately, replied, "And Dave, don't you think you had too much to do with it either. You are the eighteenth person I have called."

Late that summer someone brought me a clipping from the *Wall Street Journal* reporting Mac's sale of his firm and that he and his family had moved back to New England where he had enrolled in a distinguished school of divinity. I so hoped they would not rob Mac of his exuberant faith. His first letter encouraged me to think that he would be equal to the test. "Dave, wasn't that dreadful of that old rascal Moses to take the credit for writing the Pentateuch, for you and I know that it was Julius Wellhausen."

That retreat left its mark on all six. John resigned his enviable executive position and enrolled in a seminary in the West. After graduation and ordination, and over forty, he entered medical school where he now is preparing for psychiatry. Two of us at that retreat were ministers, and the other one, as a result of the retreat, felt led to leave the ministry. He told me that when he informed his congregation they praised God for the unexpected blessing. There are many ways by which God can get water out of rock.

When I started out as a minister-writer I soon had my lap full of pink rejection slips. Robert Frost gave me some comfort when he confided to an audience that he too had come up against a wall of rejection slips twenty years long and twenty years high. He raged, "If they won't take my poetry in the mail, I'll cram it down their throats." I believe that Frost himself would have said that it takes more than undaunted perseverance, even more than merit. It takes a break.

Several years ago my wife had mailed my sermon on the Lord's Prayer to two magazines, to *Reader's Digest* and later to *Life*. Didn't I say hope was reckless? The manuscript was returned twice. Then we wrote again to an editor of *Life*, inquiring whether they ever used an unsolicited editorial from outside their staff. This time I received a personal letter graciously informing us that the *Life* staff had been writing their own editorials since the founding of the magazine. Something in me made me fire back the now curling leaves of my Lord's Prayer sermon to a more senior editor.

Two weeks later, after I had dismissed this matter from my mind, my wife and I were discussing our need for about seven hundred dollars. In fact, we had reached the place where we had to have that sum or abandon a dream that had long been dear to our hearts. That Thursday evening we knelt down by our chairs in the living room and asked God for the money.

The next afternoon, when I was studying in the library of the University of Cincinnati beside one of those exasperating signs that shout "Silence," I thought I heard my name being paged. That was strange because I have never before or since asked for or received that courtesy in a library. "Mr. Redding, you have a long distance call at the desk." The voice at the other end of the line belonged to the editor of *Life* to whom I had first written. "Mr. Redding, we like your piece on the Lord's Prayer, and we want to publish it as our Easter editorial. Would an honorarium of $750.00 be acceptable to you?"

I replied that it would. The next Easter the *Reader's Digest*, with no further word from me, reprinted the *Life* editorial they too had originally rejected. All my writing since has resulted really from the door that opened to me there. That experience taught me that to hope is to count on far more help than one has a right or reason to expect.

Hope will simply never say die. Carl Sandburg's minister in *Remembrance Rock* was saying that "if any person knew reasons why the said parties should not be united in the holy bond of matrimony to let it be known or forever after hold his peace." The young blacksmith at this point rose to shout, "I object, I object!" The minister asked him what his objection was. He shouted seriously, earnestly, righteously, and as though it were the most proper thing in the world, "I want the girl myself! I want the girl myself!"

There is a point where hope becomes pathological, but it

won't take no for an answer until it must. And that never
kills hope; that simply dissolves one hope.

The way hope works is often comical. Hope can cut
across our best laid plans to deliver blessings ahead of
schedule, more than dreams could imagine. Hope is famous
for turning cries of despair into famous last words. Aged
Abraham was promised descendants, but when his octoge-
narian wife, Sarah, was told she was expecting, she laughed.
One has to be willing to be made a fool of to have hope, for
hope frequently comes the very way we swore it never could.

In *The Diary of Anne Frank*, the play of that starving
but delightful little sprite of courage who met her death in
the concentration camp of the Nazis, there is a surprising
tribute to hope's versatility. Near the end of the play, when
Anne and her Jewish parents hear the Gestapo breaking
down the door of their attic hiding place, Otto Frank rallies
them: "For the past two years we have lived in fear; now
we can live in hope."

Hope is a prayer beyond all hope. Not long ago my
brother-in-law, Paul, phoned to report that his young wife,
Eileen, my wife's sister, had fallen unconscious in the
kitchen and the ambulance had just taken her to the hospital. The family gathered that night to hear the neuro-
surgeon's preliminary report. "She has had an aneurysm in
the brain, and I am surprised she has survived this long."
The physician penciled a sketch to show how a weak place
in an artery had inflated, then ruptured. "Many, after such
a stroke, never make it to the hospital. If she does last the
night, in the next day or so as soon as the bleeding stops,
we will take arteriograms to determine exactly where the
hemorrhage is and discuss the possibility of surgery."

The fourth day they took the arteriograms which pic-
tured the rupture in the right side of Eileen's brain, and it
was again bleeding. Without surgery she would die, and
with surgery there was a chance. Paul chose surgery. My
wife, Dorothy, had just been reading about the actress,

Patricia Neal, who after an aneurysm had miraculously survived brain surgery and a long coma. She was then going through a tormenting siege of months of rehabilitation and was gradually beginning to keep only the names and faces of her family straight. Dorothy knew Eileen could face the same future if she lived.

St. Vincent Charity Hospital in Cleveland had just completed a new floor for neurological patients only. A team of specialists under the noted Dr. Edward Bishop had recently been organized with the latest equipment to handle the delicate operations of the brain. However, the patients we later saw there in intensive care who had survived brain surgery were not yet as fortunate as Patricia Neal, but moaned listlessly in various stages of incoherence and vegetable existence. In the intensive care room of the first hospital where Eileen had been taken lay a twenty-one-year-old boy. He too had had an aneurysm in the brain and had been operated on sometime before, but his parents and the staff had been unable to elicit any response. He lay prostrate and open-mouthed, his only movements involuntary.

Eileen, with Paul at her side, was moved slowly by ambulance from the hospital where she had been taken the night of her stroke to St. Vincent Charity for surgery. Her sister, Dorothy, followed in a car, sobbing and yet praying these unlikely words over and over again: "My strength is made *perfect* in weakness." She was not yearning only that Eileen would live, but praying that her brain would not be damaged or her body paralyzed. It seemed to me quite a large order for God to fill.

The operation began at three o'clock that afternoon. Both Paul and Dorothy phoned friends for prayers. We waited. Dinner time came and went. No word from upstairs. Eight, nine, finally ten o'clock. We were alone in the waiting room, except for a wonderful friend who worked in admissions at the hospital and who had been sent as an angel to smooth out the red tape and offer us every thoughtfulness, and another dear friend who had come from Cincinnati to be with us. At eleven P.M. the doctor sent for Paul. He walked very straight, I thought. The elevator doors closed behind him.

In a short time he burst from the elevator, face glowing, crying, "Praise the Lord!"

My wife also went up to see Eileen and returned in amazement. "Eileen's talking a mile a minute, clear as a bell. I think she tried out all the big words she knows on me just to prove her brain's undamaged. She told me, 'The doctor says I am enunciating very distinctly, and after talking with me he went out shaking his head.' She asked me if Marcia remembered her piano lesson today. Dr. Bishop insists she came through perfectly—no paralysis, no brain damage, and she is already the talk of the hospital. The only trouble with her speech is that her teeth are chattering, since they brought her temperature down into the eighties for the operation. She sounds as though they planted a computer in her brain."

Instead of the customary four to six weeks in the hospital, Eileen was up and home in thirteen days for Christmas Eve with her family. She has been driving her car and looking after her family for some time now. When she thanked the doctor at her first check-up, he reminded her of the other Physician involved: "I'm not the Lord Jesus Christ."

"Woe unto him who believes in nothing. Always the impossible happens" (Carl Sandburg). "More things are wrought by prayer than this world dreams of. Wherefore let thy voice rise . . ." (Alfred Tennyson, *Idylls of the King*).

We do not always get precisely what we pray for. Even Christ Jesus in Gethsemane had to drink the bitter cup that he had prayed, until the blood came, would go away. Yet even there, and after it seemed too late, God took away the cup in three days, granting in an even more stunning exhibition of his power exactly what Christ had prayed for.

Job never received the answers to the questions he raised. Instead of answers, God came.

Christ's temptation proved that we cannot pray for forty days and nights without ministering angels coming. If we pray tonight, some of us will find they'll come before morning. When they come, they'll bring what we want in such superior form we may have trouble recognizing our fulfilled requests at first. God may deny us our petition; he will never deny us himself. "If any of you were asked by his son for bread would you be likely to give him a stone, . . . If you then, for all your evil, . . . give good things to your children, how much more likely is it that your Heavenly Father will give good things to those who ask him?" (Matt. 7:12, Phillips).

We do not hope simply that we shall be nursed gently down to death's door. Our hope is not limited to begging for temporary relief and tortured delays to the inevitable. We hope on our dying day, as we do each night, for that which is completely impossible for man, and we shall not be disappointed.

14

CLOWNING

Lazarus Laughed *was Eugene O'Neill's play about Lazarus's* reaction to Jesus' raising him from the dead. What would happen to a man if he lost the withering fear of death and became intoxicated with the love of life beyond? According to the playwright, that heady perspective put Lazarus in a rare good humor. Laughter reversed the aging process. The years fell swiftly from this man of fifty until he was bright as a boy again.

Lazarus brought back a mysterious new dimension to laughter, rich with an unprecedented resonance, highly infectious to anyone near him, even breaking up his enemies against their will. The home of Lazarus became known as the house of laughter where men abandoned themselves to the approach of joy. The Roman threat of capital punishment and the prospect of dying again only delighted this happy man whom hope had captured.

Laughter can cut, but that is humor in reverse, as giggling may be its infancy. "How can you smile at a time like

140

this?" King Henry II asked Queen Eleanor as he was about to imprison her again. She replied: "That is the way I register despair." [1]

The comic streak in us is not necessarily our frivolous side. Even Aristotle recognized wit as wise defense against melancholy. We must go further to appreciate that pure mirth requires maturity. Laughter is not light stuff but the most serious approach to life we can make. It is easier to write tragedy than to reach a happy ending that rings true. To transport a man from depression to high spirits is a triumph of hope. Laughter is as deep and rises as high as human experience goes. Joy may spell heaven for us better than any other word or mood.

Once upon a time many churchgoers suspected that anything funny was subversive. Yesterday's pilgrim didn't care to clown, so Plymouth squeezed itself into a poker face. We are always photographed smiling "cheese," but a Puritan Winthrop wouldn't unlace a smile even for his heirloom portrait. Goodness was scrambled with solemnity. They were not as dreadful as we are determined to make them for they knew where frivolity led. Yet the shrunken Calvinist was so afraid of fun's consequences that he tried, at his fanatic worst, to wipe off every smile, put a stop to merriment, and turn off the organ music. He wouldn't let artists play with color in stained glass.

Critics unjustly trace to Jesus the depressing graveyard atmosphere that sometimes haunts the church. The men who really killed joy wore tall hats and buckled shoes. "The parsonical voice, the thin damp smell of stone," as British architect Hugh Casson calls it, were flung like a pall over the faith by some of Cromwell's men. Perhaps this grinning generation doesn't respect its forefathers enough, but those grim graybeards do deserve the blame for taking the fun out of religion.

Christ was simply not cut from black cloth no matter how the Pharisees dressed him down. The Gospels give us a

warm friend full of life, laughter, and such good news that
it showered radiance on the heads of saints and sinners alike.
According to John, he made a point of coming out at a
wedding and of deliberately turning water into wine. Jesus
derived such immense enjoyment from life he was criticized
for being a glutton and a winebibber.

It was the Pharisees, long-faced, fasting, frowning, who
always appeared to be in perpetual mourning; Christ's men
behaved like a feasting bridal party. He asked those who
scorned his merrymaking "Can ye make the children of
the bridechamber fast, while the bridegroom is with them?"
(Luke 5:34). How could men stand around like sticks in
the brilliant presence of the hope of the world? There is
much more to Christianity than skipping along blithely,
but neither can it always keep in marked military step.
Christ was born in a burst of angelic "Joy to the World."
When he came back triumphant from the fight with death,
there was such heavenly light, such overwhelming evidence
of his resurrection and life shining about him that men trem-
bled in vicarious ecstasy.

Certainly life was not too sweet to Christ. It flew at him
in a tantrum, flung suffering in his face, and hung him up to
die; but he took life and taught it a thing or two. Nothing
could destroy Christ's good humor although life tried everything. Past-master death at last had lost a man. That called
for a celebration! The last meal of the condemned man was
not taken smiling bravely through his tears but as a victory
banquet. In fact, there is so much Christmas cheer in his
achievement, we have never stopped celebrating and never
will stop as long as "we eat this bread and drink this cup."

Everyone knows that death did something terrible to
Christ, but not everyone knows he did something wonderful
to death. Men keep missing the punch line of the old, old
story. The Resurrection was relevant enough to stop Mary
Magdalene's tears, to switch desolate disciples into ecstatic
ones, and to send them out stammering with faith, in jail

and out, living or dying. After five terrible beatings and two horrible stonings, Paul, Christianity's most penalized apostle, got up and dusted off the opposition with a shout, "Rejoice in the Lord alway: and again I say, Rejoice!" (Phil. 4:4). After wading through inquisition, torture, blood and hell, the Book ends with a great host no man can number singing "Hallelujah!" As Dr. Harry E. Fosdick has said, "There is enough tragedy in the New Testament to make it the saddest book in the world and instead it is the joyfulest." [2]

There was something to laugh about before Christ's time, but doomed men do not feel much like laughing. Sometimes the happy man depresses the despairing man further. However high we rate the world's other religions, none scores very high in merriment. They regard life with varying shades of disappointment. Buddhism recommends the philosophical equivalent of slow suicide; Hinduism is too vague and Islam too fierce to find anything very amusing; but the Westminster Cathechism exuberantly claims that the chief end of man is to glorify God and *enjoy* him forever. We sing in our Doxology "Him praise with *mirth* . . ." To produce laughter in gales and peals takes more than bread enough to go around; it takes trust in a loving father. If we believe, we will find ourselves humming, and we will feel free enough from the curse of unrelieved guilt and grief to sing the humorous side of life.

Humor is built into creation. Mother Nature can be a scream. Jungle life can act up like an ape and sass us like a parrot. Disney did not originate the heavens and the earth; that was done by the same one who produced Disney's sense of humor. The model skunk was not drawn without a smile. Dr. George Buttrick believes that, "No somber God could ever have made a bullfrog or a giraffe . . . and a row of penguins looks for all the world like a speaker's table." [3] Who can keep a straight face watching little lambs scampering about stiff-legged, or baboons itching? Hearts are breaking all around us. God knows, for he gets blamed, but sides are splitting too.

Someone has been up to something, even on the deathbed. Phyllis McGinley quotes Oscar Wilde as saying, "I am dying as I lived, beyond my means." Remember Sir Thomas More's parting remark to his executioner? "Assist me up, if you please. Coming down I can shift for myself." Even when we are at the bottom of our morale, hope bubbles over and spoils the misery. Some ramrod usher spills the offering on the marble chancel floor, or some pious cleric solemnly intones the Scripture reading, ". . . and there will be sailing and gnashing of teeth." Life doubles us up in laughter as in pain, and it is in pain that Christians remember how the Lord promised, "Blessed are ye that weep now: for ye shall laugh" (Luke 6:21).

Our faith enables a man to laugh at himself. If taken in the right way, Christianity brings relief from wearisome self-inflation. Someone whose hopes are safe and sure in the hands of God and who likes to see his neighbor have a good time will come down from his pedestal and enjoy the joke he himself is. Hope can laugh when it falls down, for it knows it won't be buried there. Several old guards back at Princeton for their sixtieth reunion laughed at the souvenir combs they received, for they believed their baldness was not the last word. Robert Frost said, "Forgive, O Lord, my little jokes on Thee/And I'll forgive Thy great big one on me." [4]

Christian joy is not complete, however, until men surrender unconditionally to God. Gabriel Marcel's entry in his diary, printed in his *Being and Having*, discloses this ecstasy:

> March 5. I have no more doubts. This morning's happiness is miraculous. For the first time I have clearly experienced grace. A terrible thing to say, but it is so. I am hemmed in at last by Christianity—in, fathoms deep. Happy to be so!

. . . feel I am stammering childishly . . . this is indeed a birth. Everything is different.[5]

Christian joy is not passed out with the Sunday bulletins; it blooms from the dedicated life. The sweets of the faith, God's friendship and forgiveness, the only fun that's any good and clean, lie around lifeless and dormant until we are sworn in. It was not until St. Francis gave himself up to God, silver and soul, that he started singing and dancing in the streets. Why don't we have strength to carry a tune? Could it be that nothing ever broke our ego's ice to make us burst with music?

A new birth, Christ said. Until that old native stone is pried loose, laughter will be derived from swapping dirty jokes. It is the decision to do the will of God that gives us wings to meet and embrace the joy coming down from heaven. That is what unclenches the tight Zacchean fist; that is what makes us cut and serve our little piece of property with irrepressible generosity. The report of our change will go up like a cheer from all the King's men.

For what really brightens the Christian house is not the arrival of the righteous but the homecoming of the damned. The Christian's keenest hopes are not concentrated in the mirror but on the dark horses least expected to cross the finish line. Nothing is more fun than pulling those practical jokes on the devil—fooling Wormwood's agents by smuggling out men given up for dead. A man who is alive can laugh, but laughter is a love story that dotes on another's rescue best of all. The good shepherd gets more excited over finding one stray lamb than bringing in the ninety-nine. The prodigal's father did not celebrate the boy who stayed behind; the sight that made him shout for joy was of the lad he'd never given up hoping for coming toward him over the horizon. Nothing makes heaven half as happy as these surprise comebacks.

Heaven has its hopes pinned on the odd man out, the planet nobody thought would make it. When the sun seems blotted out, could it be covered with caps tossed high in triumph by the great host of witnesses for some black sheep's victory against great odds below? ". . . I tell you, there will be more joy in heaven over one sinner who repents . . ." (Luke 15:7, RSV).

15

HOPE
FIGHTS

Hope works through us. To interpret hope as waiting idly for God to do everything is to make a vile caricature of this energetic virtue. Our hope is in God's return to finish what he started, but this does not put anybody out of work. It creates peak employment. God's Kingdom has just the job waiting for every man, and only those who misunderstand ever misuse the hand of God as unemployment compensation.

However, laziness is not solely a bad habit, but so often results from fatiguing hopelessness. The victim's resources are all consumed forever in fighting that losing battle that began long ago. The listless or the sticklers for the status quo may have a conflict or sore spot that is bleeding away their incentive.

The celestial target date set by Christianity does not sidetrack one from labor; it gives a man something to work for. It makes him important. He is going places. His effort will amount to something. The man who believes that it is

147

futile will lie down on the job, just as one who is convinced that he is in the pay of God will be an inspired man of action.

"We want you out there marching with us in the picket line tomorrow. The blacks have good reason to be violent about this city's stupor. No local bank will grant them a mortgage and ghetto landlords charge whatever rent they please for the blacks are forced to live there. If you and others like you don't stand up and be counted, this seething hole soon will explode with their resentment." My fellow ministers were ready for action and had come to recruit me.

"I'm sorry," I said. "I know something has to be done immediately, but I cannot do that."

"Are you afraid, or are you a standpatter?" "Neither, I hope, but neither am I going to be impressed into inflaming the race problem further as I am afraid this approach will do." "Then what are you going to do?"

That was a good question, one I and other social moderates could not put off answering. At that time I was a minister in a large urban church in a midwestern city certainly destined, without rapid social action, for racial turbulence. From the previous experience I have shared, I had lost confidence in petitioning and picketing which are fringe rights under our constitution and can so often be exercised out of guilt or in sophomoric desperation rather than in sound hope. Yet I deeply believed in fair play and I knew that the blacks in our town had seldom had it.

What could I do, and what could our church do that would be in character and unite us in a crisis that was dividing so many congregations into sterile splinters of controversy? It is a sin to despise the urban situation as hopeless, as it is a sin to be pressured or panicked onto someone else's bandwagon as the only way out. A Christian has confidence that he will be shown what he is to do. Somehow I was given hope that an opening would appear.

It did. One morning I picked up the phone and a gruff but respectful voice asked, "Are you Rev. Redding?" "Yes."

"Well, this is Charlie. I've just been paroled, and I need a job bad. Can't find no place to stay, and you told me to call you as soon as I got out." I soon realized that I was not the Rev. Redding he was after who apparently worked with ex-convicts. I received a number of such phone calls which at last succeeded in unsettling me in one respect. I did not feel ready yet for Christ to say to *me*, as he indicated he would do in the parable on the last judgment, "I was in prison, and ye came unto me" (Matt. 25:36).

Soon after this short siege of softening-up calls, which I do not believe were visited upon me by chance, I was invited to a weekly prayer luncheon led by prominent Cleveland laymen. Across the table from me sat the only other guest that day, Rev. James Redding. He was a black man. We found we saw eye to eye on the volatile urban dilemma. Providence was working with my limitations! Jim Redding and I took to each other from that time on as though God himself had arranged our meeting.

He had been trying to establish a halfway house for ex-convicts in Cleveland along the lines of the famed Dismas House founded by Father Clark in St. Louis. He had met with a succession of heartbreaking failures. Everybody raved about the idea in general, but absolutely nobody wanted a gang of interracial criminals moving in next door. The court was just then in the process of zoning him out of another house he had thought might be a last possibility.

Jim Redding is an imposing and powerful figure and, I have no doubt, will one day become one of Cleveland's legends. We organized. Jim was executive director, and he insisted that I become chairman of the Board of Directors of what was then nothing. We went around making speeches together, billing ourselves as the Redding Brothers, presenting the problems of the man just emerging from a penal institution and his need for a place to go until he had a job and a home. Without this fresh assistance the ex-con would be forced to return to his old cronies and habits and to repeat the crime and the punishment as most unassisted parolees do. The man with a bad record not only has no credit and no references; no one wants him back home. He is disowned and foot-loose except for the tempting opportunities pushed at him by the underworld.

Our "brothers" act was so successful that the Internal Revenue called Jim on the carpet to explain the questionable practice of his being in the employ of a board of directors that included his brother. Jim replied: "You mean Dave? He's no brother of mine; he's a Presbyterian."

Buildings and financial support came, and our own sedate church, which could not have weathered so many proposed solutions to the race problem, entered with warm enthusiasm into this interracial project in the Hough area. It seemed time to ask the session to invite Rev. James Redding to preach in our historic pulpit. They were unanimously in favor.

The genuine approval of the session and the congregational support we were receiving for Halfway House reassured me that this really was God's idea for us. Volunteer groups from the church had been going down on Saturdays to paint and clean. Others had donated their business and organizational abilities. I must confess, however, that as the day for Jim's pulpit appearance drew close, I developed cold feet, for we had a number of icily conservative members, and I was apprehensive in particular about one pro-segregation family.

That morning when Jim marched into the chancel with me he was carrying an embarrassingly large limb of a tree, and I noticed for the first time that all the exits were distressingly distant from the pulpit!

Jim preached powerfully that day and not too long on what God could do with a crooked tree such as the one he waved so effectively overhead to the immense interest of the children. I know, for he has since told me, that he regarded that morning as one of the biggest moments of his life, and his sermon was one of the most moving I have ever heard. After the benediction, I braced myself beside him at the door to get the reaction from our cultivated congregation. My segregationist family got to us first. They are the only family I can remember coming out of the church that day. The wife took Jim's big hand in both her own and, with the tears still glistening on her cheeks, she said, "Why Rev. Redding, I haven't heard preaching like that since I was a little girl." She saw *me* standing there, too!

When I resigned from my post at that church not so long after that, one of our finest but most conservative church leaders pledged a monthly gift to Halfway House in my name until such time as it was on solid financial ground. Two of our churchmen became board members; the church budgets money and sends work crews for the cause.

When the riots came to Cleveland that summer, it was Jim Redding whom the *Reader's Digest* for May, 1967, hailed in a feature article as "the man who stopped the riot." All of this experience was to me the realization not of idle wishful thinking but of our dedicated hope in God constructively working out solutions.

When one thinks about the prospects for good ever being able to triumph in general over the forces of evil, it all appears as hopeless as the headlines, but this kind of abstraction is an evil distraction from our specific duty. We are to leave to God the saving of the world, and you and I are to concentrate on the God-given job to which each has been assigned. We are not to preoccupy ourselves with God's overall worries. We are to do his will today where we are. This close-up focus yields hope.

Hope is applying our future security to present problems. Hope results in solid and creative action. Much social action, for instance, is not only divisive, but it is hit-and-run. It is little better than a fraternity antic or Halloween prank, and will wash off with the next rain. Neither the plan nor the deed was born of God, but aborted in men who are doing it with malice aforethought, perhaps in adolescent retaliation against offenders who oppose them. But a good deed is on a ground swell, and it magnetizes and unites without disdain all the elements for good.

One of the developments that flowered through Rev. James Redding led to my being contacted by men still in the penitentiary who were trying to work out their parole plan. One very articulate correspondent who had been imprisoned for pushing drugs continued to write to me consistently for two years. Finally he informed me that he had been released. It was the week before Christmas. My wife and teen-age daughter felt we should invite him for Christmas day. He called Christmas morning to thank us but to explain that he was paroled to the city limits of Columbus: "I was thrown out of the pen with the dishwater with only three dollars left to last me until I get a job. Can you help me?"

I told him, "I am hard-pressed at the moment myself, trying to feed four children among other things, but I'll see what I can do." However, after we had all opened our Christmas presents that morning, we sat picturing him in his YMCA room alone, and God prompted the two women in my family once more. "Why not make the hour-and-a-half drive down to Columbus and take him out for Christmas dinner?" This same spell was cast over my three boys, whom I couldn't have imagined leaving their new Christmas toys even if the Russians were coming. "You can have my new silver dollar, Dad, to help with dinner." The rest brought theirs. I sensed that my Christmas dinner, perhaps Christmas itself, was waiting in Columbus.

Jon emerged, distinguished looking, from the elevator of the YMCA. For the first time I realized he was a black. "We're here to take you out to dinner." "No," he objected, "I'm taking *you*, and I've already made the reservations." I was staggered, and began to be ashamed for presuming that this man would naturally squeeze me out of all he could.

He explained, "You said you had a large family and lots of Christmas bills so I saw this notice in the elevator offering a free Christmas dinner, and a Mr. and Mrs. Daniels at Freedom Heritage House are expecting us." After my surprise and shame subsided, I began to be disappointed for having to sacrifice dinner at a fine restaurant for welfare cooking.

The address took us into the black ghetto. We walked by unsold Christmas trees at the front entrance and pressed the doorbell. An attractive black woman came to the door and welcomed us all for Christmas dinner. She had been looking for us. As soon as I saw her and her husband, I knew we had come to the right place. They were gracious and cultured, an unforgettable story in themselves. They were both college graduates. He had studied at the Sorbonne, and had had an audience with President Roosevelt. They had lived next door to this house, lamenting the deterioration of their neighborhood as well as the vacancy of this decaying mansion. They had taken a leap of faith, made a down payment, and opened classes in homemaking, baby care, job training, typing, and remedial reading. "So far we have been able to meet the payments," they stated with pride. Now we too had landed in their arms, and they have since grown incredibly dear to us as well as being a lifesaver to Jon. He had no one in Columbus. Now he had the Daniels.

That was a Christmas dinner our family never will forget. Such food! We were late, so most of the other guests had already come and gone. We laughed and talked so much you would have thought we belonged together. As we rose to leave, Mrs. Daniels suggested we make a prayer circle. I never knew how my group of little men would respond when you say "pray" in public, but there was a glory on us that night. Each prayed manfully for God to bless Jon when it came his turn. The ex-convict was next to last. I had been wondering what was going through Jon's mind and whether he would pass. He whispered a sentence hoarsely that has stayed with me: "There's only one Person know how I really feel just now. Amen."

None of us can prescribe a course of action for another person, but controversial issues must not confound us into inactivity. We must address each other to God. Dynamic hope will single out your job in the very situation now confronting you. You will not be put to work chipping paint, or running errands for someone else's idea of having a good time. Your task will be just right for you, thrilling, satisfying, and expanding into something else without the bad side effects of LSD.

That tattered bloody flag for peace still waves, and we listen for the sound of the last cannon. We wait for someone to work for a new kind of soldier to outwit war, that vicious old-timer. Here's where the next generation shines us to shame. We're right to be worried about hippies who hog the headlines, but the young people today in the Peace Corps and in a shower of unsung services have accomplished more in the cause of brotherhood than all the youth in your day and mine together. A woman about my age exposed the awful way we were taught to look after old number one in our own youth when she complained about youngsters going into the Peace Corps, "Aren't they thinking about their future?" How much better if we had been working on the future in the way our boys and girls are now. It may take a little girl armed with hope to disarm a world. Carl Sandburg stated the case for that child eloquently in his line from *The People Yes:* "Sometime they'll give a war and nobody will come." [1]

The coming of the Kingdom is no escapist exit from responsible citizenship. Poverty, race, and air pollution may be overpopularized at the expense of an invisible sea of miseries on the highway and in the nursing home, but they are beginnings. A proliferation of plans are presently afoot for tackling troubles which unorganized men could never solve. If there is no planning there is no realistic hope, and many are on the side of the angels, whether they know it or not. Giving the disadvantaged youngster a head start or offering the dropout a viable alternative to crime is what hope is made for.

With hope we not only think of possibilities, we organize to see them through—to see that no one is locked out of a house, bank, or office because of his color, creed, or sex. You cannot sweat something out without a tenacious hope it will work out.

All the Kingdom's men will be distinguished from busy-bodies and troublemakers by their stimulus. The man who has Christ's hope will never impose his joy roughly as a self-appointed task; he will come to it reverently as a vocation to which he has been divinely ordained, and he will not take the credit for the fruits of his labors.

Hope does not deteriorate into acts of desperation, but burns brighter brainstorms as the need arises. My father, a strange mixture of frontiersman and baseball player who became a Methodist circuit rider, was old enough to be my grandfather. He wasn't much better than I at waiting, but he illustrated, as well as anyone I know, hope working in emergencies with sanctified imagination. He never reached the extremity where there was nothing he could do. When things went haywire, he would work something out with a pair of pliers. Dad never wasted his breath mouthing platitudes; he found solutions.

One winter when he was logging he lost his two thermos jugs. He never said a word, but kept his weather eye open until he was sure who the two pilferers were. They lived in a tumbledown shack just over the hill from us. One Saturday Dad dropped by their shack shortly after the boys had left for town. A hard-pressed woman came to the door and eyed him suspiciously. Dad swept off his hat in his most expansive manner: "I'm awfully glad to have the chance to meet you." Then he added offhandedly, "I just dropped by to pick up the thermos jugs I lent the boys." She disappeared and returned in a minute with the loot. Dad waved away her thanks and left with his property, as if bringing that off were all in a day's work.

Dad never became senile but kept sharp by practicing on emergencies. One time when he was in his sixties, he was driving down hair-raising Pine Grove hill at the point where it has dumped many cars into Yellow Creek in southeast Ohio's anonymous mountains. The brakes failed on his old transmission-troubled 1929 Chevy. My twelve-year-old cousin who was with him never forgot that drag strip, nor how cool my father kept. Dad managed to double-clutch the car into second without securing any detectable slowing action. The car was careening much too quickly for the fast cuts that road takes, so Dad eased the fenders up against the slender guard rail tighter and tighter until it slowed them down. Then it was back out in the road again until the remedy had to be repeated. It never occurred to him to stop the car and walk to the village garage. Dad never thanked himself for the solutions the God of hope had helped him work out.

The story of Joseph and his brothers illustrates how God can make his hopes come true, even from devil's work. C. S. Lewis insisted that no one can outwit God; those who refuse to be God's servants shall become his tools. The busier the devil gets, the quicker he plays into God's hand. Joseph's brothers sold Joseph off to Egypt. He was as good as dead. But God put Joseph to work at Pharoah's side saving enough corn to feed the children of Israel who were famished by the time they arrived. Joseph forgave those murderers in words that should reassure the frantic nations now that there is someone God enough to use hell against itself: "But as for you, ye thought evil against me; but God meant it unto good . . ." (Gen. 50:20).

We could use a Joseph in Moscow now to say nothing of New York. Faith declares that God will not discriminate against us. He will pick men to outwit the famine approaching now. Stalin's daughter has become one of the great Christian converts of modern times. The world has gone to hell in the headlines and in the most modern hotel registers. The speed of the space age is so good at hiding sin that it has spun the story of the traveling salesman completely out of moral control—expense accounts can be neatly padded to include an illicit overnight partner. And yet let us not surrender to hell so hastily. This contaminated world at its worst is where God walks in.

Bill Glass, professional football star, related to me an incident in the life of one of the wealthiest men in America. This industrialist had long been intrigued by Christianity but had cautiously kept it at arm's length. At a recent luncheon, however, his wife had confessed her faith to their guests, and shortly thereafter his daughter had phoned from school that she had been moved to become a Christian.

After a week in Switzerland spent on business with a devout Christian, the industrialist turned in exasperation to the vice-president who had accompanied him. "I'm going out on the town to forget. I'm having religious claustrophobia. Will you come with me?" The vice-president, who happened also to have become a Christian, sighed, "I'll go with you," not knowing what he was in for.

That evening at a night club the rich man noticed the loveliest call girl sitting at the bar alone and promptly invited her to their table. To his dismay, the girl immediately began bestowing her attentions upon the dedicated vice-president. She was trying excitedly to say something in beautiful gestures and broken English. Finally the man made it out: "Your face," she said, "eez like ze Billee Graham." Soon she had radiantly confided that she had been converted in a recent crusade. She was only remaining on her job because she felt ethically obliged to do so until her contract expired in another two weeks. God can turn up anywhere and stop at nothing to get his man or woman.

Jesus was a politico-messianic member of the royal family of David, wearing the title Prince of Peace. This hope has never been a purely private matter; it has been *our* hope with far-reaching civic duties ever since the example of Jeremiah.

For God's hope to come true, our country must carry out what our forefathers envisioned for a nation under God. Have we forgotten that the father of our country prayed at Valley Forge as earnestly as the savior of the country prayed over Bull Run? Washington was one general who asked his soldiers not to swear: "How can we expect the blessing of Providence upon our arms if we insult it by our impiety?" Our textbooks may have been forced to delete the gigantic part God played in the creation of our country, but he was so noticeable even the Colonial army and the Congress detected him as their champion. At the National Convention, Benjamin Franklin spoke:

> Mr. President . . . I have lived sir, a long time, and the longer I live, the more convincing proofs I see of this truth— that God governs in the affairs of men. And if a sparrow cannot fall to the ground without His notice, is it probable that an empire can rise without His concurring aid? . . . Except the Lord build the house they labor in vain that build it . . . I therefore . . . move that henceforth prayers imploring the assistance of heaven . . . be held in this assembly every morning.

Our national purpose is easy to sing, but to "be true to thee 'til death" will take some doing. Our official documents anticipate our coming up with something more than a mere survival technique. We will have to do something better than be the best bomb makers the world has ever seen, if we are to avoid the epitaph that hangs over the ashes of so many other vain attempts, "the almost-chosen people." Our national hope hangs on the scarlet thread of whether we can bring down to earth his dreams of a Kingdom.

It still remains to be seen whether our government is

godlier than the Communist regime. We say it is but the world will not take our word for it. We have a lot to live up to in Vietnam, in Detroit, in Times Square, and in outer space.

One of our finest patriots was the late Henry Luce, famed founder and editor of the *Life*, *Time*, and *Fortune* publishing empire. He never became so buried beneath the bad news happening around us that he forgot the good news that ought to be happening to and through "this Pilgrim people." He was able to fascinate the readers of *Life* with a series of sermons featuring our national purpose.

"The magazines," he urged his editors, "should reflect the belief that human life is tragic and triumphant and also comic, but never as Sartre proclaims, absurd." [2] His patriotism was not a "blind attachment to geography" but devotion to that finer destiny instilled in him by his missionary parents:

> An American can't take his Americanism for granted . . . He has to criticize it because it is a proposition—an ideal ever seeking incarnation . . . This has been the country of easy answers . . . of the endless frontier, of the big sky, of manifest destiny, of unlimited resources, of go west young man, of opportunity for all, of rags to riches, mass production, nothing to fear but fear itself, technical know-how, a chicken in every pot, gung ho and can do . . . we have won all the marbles and it just isn't enough. Further, the United States of America knows or feels that it isn't enough. [3]

Luce never recommended that we compete with Russia for a man-made Utopia. He challenged this land of plenty with a quest reminiscent of the ancient one that almost four thousand years ago raised Abraham's sights from Ur: "To create on this continent . . . the first modern technological, prosperous, humane and reverent civilization." [4]

We must go on from there to add that the promise was for all nations. Israel was to be no spoiled pet but an industrious servant so that "in thee shall all families of the

earth be blessed" (Gen. 12:3). China is as precious to
God as Chicago or the Congo. Our hope is not exclusive of
the wildlife, but concerned for the destiny of mankind. It
is not his will "that one of these little ones should perish"
(Matt. 18:14).

God is tired of being introduced unimaginatively as a
specialist only in creation. Luke's fifteenth chapter corrects
that one-sidedness with the stories of the lost sheep, the lost
coin, and the lost son, which introduced a God of consummation. The three parables underline his re-creation—the
God who is in maintenance and repair, both competent and
busy in the final stages of completion. It is high time we saw
the Creator as the finisher of our faith, fascinated with any
new business of finding lost pieces of planets and men.
"Ninety-nine are not enough to God," said Cardinal John
Wright.

This hope of ours is happening in history, if not in the
history book. Our prayer does not stop short of the world of
work that we are to do in the beloved words left too long
upon our lips, "Thy Kingdom come on *earth* as it is in
heaven."

We already occupy front seats at the site God has selected
for the eschatological wonder to take place. Christians are
not spiritualists any more than they are materialists. Earth,
like Kittyhawk, is a field for landing as well as for taking
off.

> But God's own descent
> Into flesh was meant
> As a demonstration
> That the supreme merit
> Lay in risking spirit
> In substantiation
> Spirit enters flesh
> And for all it's worth
> Charges into earth.[5]

It is not God's intention to abandon earth as a bad job
and take us away from all this to an escape-hatch heaven.

He is recapturing this planet with our help, preparatory to moving heaven in.

Christ is expected to return and remain. Our hope is not up in the air but grounded in the redemptive developments completing earth's restoration. The crooked shall be made straight in our calendars—that is, *our* lamb shall have nothing to fear from the wolf, for the wolf and the lamb shall feed side by side, not in distant Elysian fields, but in *our* pastures and in *our* barns. *Your* child and mine will be playing, safe from harm, in what used to be the horror of the adder's den. ". . . the earth shall be full of the knowledge of the Lord . . ." (Isa. 11:9).

All of the pieces from broken hearts, every fragment of man's lost and forgotten dreams, will be swept up and restored in the splendor of an even holier night, emerging from the shadow of hard times in the old life we led. "And I saw a new heaven and a *new earth:* for the first heaven and the first earth were passed away . . ." (Rev. 21:1). "Fondly do we hope, fervently do we pray." [6]

NOTES

CHAPTER ONE

1. William Graham Cole, *The Restless Quest of Modern Man* (New York: Oxford University Press, 1966), p. 60. Used by permission.
2. *Time*, 25 July 1969, pp. 64–65.
3. John Calvin, *Institutes*, III, 2:42.
4. Pelegrin, *And a Time to Die.*

CHAPTER TWO

1. *Time*, 8 August 1969, p. 30.

CHAPTER THREE

1. Elsa Morante, *Arthuro's Island*, trans. Isabel Quigley (London: Wm. Collins Sons & Co., Ltd., 1959), pp. 135–36.
2. William F. Lynch, *Images of Hope* (Baltimore: Helicon, 1965). Used by permission.
3. Ibid.
4. Leo Tolstoy, *Anna Karenina* (New York: New American Library, 1961), p. 528.
5. T. S. Eliot, *The Family Reunion* (New York: Harcourt, Brace & World, 1967), p. 252.

CHAPTER FOUR

1. Lynch, *Images of Hope.*
2. Ibid., p. 176.
3. Boris Pasternak, *Dr. Zhivago* (New York: Pantheon Books, a Division of Random House, Inc., 1958), p. 402. Used by permission.

CHAPTER FIVE

1. From "Elijah" by Felix Mendelssohn.

CHAPTER SIX

1. Amando Zegri.

CHAPTER SEVEN

1. Robert Bolt, *A Man for All Seasons* (New York: Vintage Books, 1962), p. 81.
2. St. Augustine, *Augustine: Confessions*, Great Books, Encyclopedia Britannica (Chicago: William Benton, 1952), p. 19.

CHAPTER EIGHT

1. Jürgen Moltmann, *Theology of Hope* (New York: Harper & Row, 1965), p. 30.

CHAPTER TEN

1. Gabriel Marcel, *Being and Having* (New York: Harper & Row, London: Dacre Press, A. & C. Black, Ltd., 1962), p. 37.
2. Tennessee Williams, *The Rose Tattoo* (New York: New Directions, 1951), pp. viii, x.
3. Reprinted by permission of the publishers and the Trustees of Amherst College from Thomas H. Johnson, Editor, *The Poems of Emily Dickinson*, Cambridge, Mass.: The Belknap Press of Harvard University Press, copyright, 1951, 1955, by The President and Fellows of Harvard College.
4. Quoted by Samuel Keen, *Christian Century*, 26 January 1967, p. 108.
5. Marcel, *Homo Viator*, pp. 147, 162.
6. From *The Sermons of Phillips Brooks*.

CHAPTER ELEVEN

1. John Baillie, *The Idea of Progress* (New York: Scribner's Sons, 1951), p. 61. Used by permission.
2. Sir John Seely, *Ecce Homo* (New York: E. P. Dutton & Co.), p. 264.

CHAPTER TWELVE

1. Gian-Carlo Menotti, *Amahl and the Night Visitors*. Copyright 1952 by G. Schirmer Inc. Used by permission.
2. Keen, p. 108.

3. William Shakespeare, *As You Like It*, Act II, Scene 2, lines 12–20.

4. *Selected Poems of Emily Dickinson* (New York: The Modern Library, 1948), p. 73.

5. From the *Biography of George Mason*.

CHAPTER FOURTEEN

1. From the film *The Lion in Winter*.

2. Harry Emerson Fosdick, *The Manhood of the Master*, Association Press. Used by permission.

3. George Buttrick, *Sermons Preached in a University Church* (New York: Abingdon Press, 1959), p. 52. Used by permission.

4. Robert Frost, *In the Clearing* (New York: Holt, Rinehart & Winston, 1962), p. 39.

5. Marcel, *Being and Having*, p. 15.

CHAPTER FIFTEEN

1. Carl Sandburg, *The People Yes* (New York: Harcourt, 1936).

2. Henry Luce, *Life*, 10 March 1967, p. 30. *Used by permission.*

3. Ibid.

4. Ibid.

5. Frost, *In the Clearing*, frontispiece.

6. From Abraham Lincoln's Second Inaugural Address.